WHY?

• • • Answers to Everyday • • •
Scientific Questions

JOEL LEVY

35 Stillman Street, Suite 121
San Francisco, CA 94107
www.zestbooks.net

First published in the United States in 2013 by Zest Books
Copyright © 2012 by Michael O'Mara Books Limited, London

Designed by Greg Stevenson
Illustrations by Greg Stevenson, with the exception of page 28

Young Adult Nonfiction / Science & Nature / General
Library of Congress control number: 2013941857
ISBN: 978-0-9827322-9-8

Manufactured in the U.S.A.
DOC 10 9 8 7 6 5 4 3 2 1
4500437163

JOEL LEVY is a writer and journalist specializing in science and
history. He is the author of more than a dozen books, including
Poison: A Social History; *Great Scientists, Mad Science;* and
Scientific Feuds: From Galileo to the Human Genome Project,
and has also written features and articles for newspapers and
magazines. He lives in London.

Contents

Introduction

"A generous and elevated mind is distinguished by nothing more certainly than an eminent degree of curiosity." —*Samuel Johnson*

"Be not curious in unnecessary matters," the Bible declares, "for more things are showed unto thee than men understand." I respectfully disagree, and the fact that you've picked up this book suggests that your generous and elevated mind is also distinguished by a degree of curiosity. Hopefully, the answers in these pages—which range from knowledge you may have garnered from old school textbooks to unusual but true facts you're more likely to pick up from interesting anecdotes than from the *Encyclopedia Brittanica*—will reward that curiosity. Did you know, for instance, that you get heavier when you sunbathe but that when water freezes into ice, it gets lighter? Or that no one knows how long lobsters might be able to live? Or that the earth is smoother than a billiard ball? Or that, contrary to popular belief, giraffes are very chatty but talk in tones too low for us to hear?

These and many other bits of trivia—such as the number of volcanoes erupting as you read this line (around 20) to the color of the sky on Mars (red)—are revealed in the process of answering over 50 deceptively simple questions about nature.

Obviously, there are an infinite number of questions that could have been asked, so why choose this particular assortment? In selecting the questions, I have tried to cover both classic musings ("Why is the sky blue?") and ones that might not have previously occurred to you ("Why do we forget?"), from geology to psychology, from cosmology to chemistry, with questions ranging from the mundane ("Why does my cell phone lose its signal?") to the esoteric ("Why does time only move forward?").

I have tried to provide several levels or layers of explanation. Each answer begins with a one-line explanation before giving more detail and, in some instances, challenging the basic premise of the question. (For instance, did you know that there actually is no dark side of the moon?) Then the answer is given in more detail, with a fuller explanation and, where possible, some illuminating and fun trivia.

Keep in mind, when reading the answers, the difference between proximate and ultimate explanations. A proximate explanation describes the immediate, direct cause for something. For instance, ice floats because it is less dense than liquid water. But proximate explanations often invite a further question—for instance, why is ice less dense than water? This is where the ultimate explanation comes in, that details the root cause—in this case, the unique ability of water molecules to form a special type of bond with each other, which leads to the unusual properties of ice.

The search for ultimate explanations can steer us in exciting and unexpected directions, and you will see that some of the least promising questions turn out to have the most interesting answers. For example: Why are men generally bigger than women? At first glance, this doesn't appear to be the most profound or interesting question in the book, but the search for an answer leads into strange territory, taking us on a journey through the sexual habits of apes, the logic of genetic inheritance, and the importance of a father's involvement in raising girls.

Not all of the questions can be answered. Nobody really knows, for instance, why we dream or even the reason for sleep. Explanations for the expansion of the universe are only theories—informed speculation on a cosmic scale. The nature and causes of global warming are extremely contentious, and in a book of bite-sized answers, there obviously isn't enough space to do full justice to the range of opinion or evidence involved. Karl Popper pointed out that "our knowledge can only be finite, while our ignorance must necessarily be infinite," but I would prefer to leave you with the more consoling words of James Thurber: "It is better to ask some of the questions than to know all of the answers."

NATURE AND THE EARTH

Why does the sun shine?

The sun shines because it is constantly exploding—like a giant nuclear bomb.

A nuclear bomb explodes because of a process called nuclear fusion, in which the nuclei (the bits in the middle) of atoms are fused together, releasing huge amounts of energy. Some of this energy is in the form of heat and some is in the form of light. The sun is like a massive nuclear bomb exploding at every given moment, so it is constantly expelling both heat and light—so much that it warms and brightens the earth, which is 92 million miles away.

The sun is a huge ball of gas, 2,200 trillion trillion tons of it (that's a mass some 333,000 times heavier than the earth). Most of this gas is hydrogen. The enormous gravity of the sun squeezes this gas so tightly that the nuclei of the hydrogen atoms fuse together to form helium nuclei. In the process, a tiny fraction of the mass of each nucleus is converted into energy, so that the sun is exploding more fiercely than four million nuclear bombs a second!

Burning away

The sun burns through so much fuel that it loses the equivalent of a supertanker's cargo every heartbeat. Fortunately, the sun is so immense that this missing chunk of matter makes little difference. Even though it has been burning matter at this rate for billions of years, the sun has only lost 0.1 percent of its mass, and it will be another five billion years before it runs out of hydrogen for fusion.

What exactly happens in the sun during nuclear fusion? The nucleus is the hub in the center of an atom, which is normally surrounded by electrons. The intense heat of the sun strips these electrons off atoms of hydrogen, leaving behind a big soup of hydrogen nuclei. Hydrogen is the smallest and simplest element, and its nucleus consists of single nuclear particles. Under the intense gravity of the sun, four of these nuclear particles are crushed together until they fuse into a new type of atomic nucleus—a helium nucleus. During this process, the sun generates energy at about the same rate as 400 trillion power stations working at full capacity!

Only in the center of the sun can you find a gravitational pressure strong enough to trigger fusion. The sunshine we see and feel is generated by the intensely hot surface of the sun. If you heat a metal spoon to a high enough temperature, it will become white-hot and glow with intense heat and light; similarly, solar fusion is not the direct source of sunshine, but is the ultimate cause.

So if the sun is exploding with the force of more than four million nuclear bombs a second, why doesn't it fly apart? The answer is gravity. The size of the sun is the result of the balance between the outward and inward forces affecting it; in other words, gravity is pulling its matter in toward the center, while the explosive power of nuclear fusion is blasting it outward. When the sun does finally begin to run out of fuel, this balance will change and gravity will eventually triumph; the sun will end up as a white dwarf, a solidly compacted mass of atomic nuclei, gradually cooling down until it is just a dead cinder floating in space.

Why are plants green?

Plants are green because they soak up red and blue light. If you take the red and blue colors out of white light, what you are left with is the color green.

Humans and other animals get their energy by eating and digesting food, but plants make their own food by harvesting sunlight. They use the energy from sunlight to drive a chemical reaction called photosynthesis, which converts carbon dioxide and water into sugar.

Sunlight is a mixture of different colors, or wavelengths, that combine to form white light. When white sunlight falls on a leaf, the red and blue wavelengths are absorbed by a pigment called chlorophyll. A pigment is a chemical that is very good at absorbing certain wavelengths of light and reflecting others, giving it an intense color. Once the pigment has done its work, green light is all that is left to reflect back to our eyes.

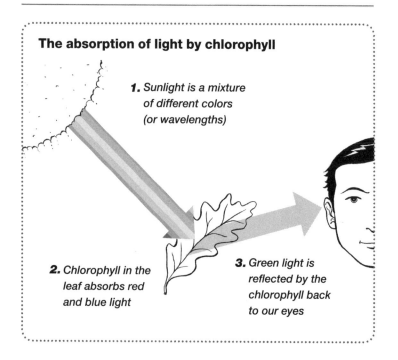

The absorption of light by chlorophyll

1. Sunlight is a mixture of different colors (or wavelengths)

2. Chlorophyll in the leaf absorbs red and blue light

3. Green light is reflected by the chlorophyll back to our eyes

Chlorophyll is a complex molecule that has evolved to capture light energy and transfer it to other molecules. It works in a similar fashion to a satellite dish you might use to pick up television signals. A satellite dish collects radio waves carrying television transmissions from a wide area and focuses them onto a single point, concentrating lots of weak signals into a strong one. Similarly, chlorophyll collects light over a wide area and concentrates the energy into a single channel. This concentrated light energy is powerful enough to drive a biochemical cycle that makes sugars, which in turn act as a kind of biochemical fuel store, easily burned by the plant's cells to release energy when it is needed.

A mammoth task

Photosynthesis is happening all the time, practically everywhere. Every year photosynthesizing plants and microbes make 105 petagrams of sugar and similar substances. That's 116 billion tons, equivalent to about 26 billion elephants—which is enough elephants to create a tower stretching to the moon and back 136 times over.

But why does chlorophyll absorb only red and blue light? If plants need light energy for photosynthesis, why don't they use a pigment that absorbs all the light? In other words, why not use a black pigment? Why are plants green and not black?

Sunlight is a mix of different colors, but it doesn't contain all the colors equally. The spectrum of light coming from the sun (the full range of wavelengths) is more intense in some bands than in others. A pigment that absorbs across all bands equally would be inefficient. It takes energy to build pigments, and the more colors the pigment has to absorb, the more energy it costs to build. Evolution favors the most efficient solution to a problem, and plants that waste energy-building pigments to absorb weak colors would be left in the dust by more efficient plants. In theory, the colors absorbed most strongly by chlorophyll are those that are most intense in sunlight. An obvious explanation for why chlorophyll reflects green and absorbs red and blue would be that red and blue are the most intense colors in the spectrum of sunshine, and green is the weakest.

In reality, the opposite is true. The most intense part of the solar spectrum is the green-yellow band. Why are most plants not using a pigment that absorbs it? No one really knows, but there are a number of possible explanations. It may be the case that the green part of sunshine is too intense, and the delicate molecules involved in photosynthesis might be damaged by it. By analogy, humans need some oxygen in the air that we breathe, but oxygen is a very reactive element and becomes toxic at high levels. If you were given 100 percent oxygen to breathe, you would die.

Another explanation is that when chlorophyll originally evolved, the earth was already dominated by microorganisms using a different pigment, called retinol, which does absorb green-yellow light, so that the dominant color of life on the planet was purple. These purple microbes soaked up all the green-yellow light, leaving only red and blue light for chlorophyll-bearing microbes to exploit.

Why are there 365 days in a year?

There are 365 days in a year because the earth makes 365 revolutions in the time it takes to go all the way around the sun.

To be precise, there are about 365.25 days in a year, according to NASA, but our calendars only make room for whole days, so the extra quarter from each year is saved up and used all at once every 4 years. This is known as a leap year, when the calendar has 366 days. The actual time it takes for the earth to go around the sun and get back to the exact same spot is 1.0000174 years.

Other planets have longer or shorter years, depending on how far out from the sun they are. Neptune is 2.8 billion miles from the sun and takes 164.79 Earth years to go around it, although its day is shorter than an Earth day (just 16 hours long) because it spins around faster. Mercury takes just 88 days to complete an orbit at a speed of 107,700 miles per hour, as it is the closest planet to the sun and experiences much greater gravitational pull. However, Earth is no slouch: In a year it travels 587.5 million miles around the sun at about 67,000 mph.

The earth didn't always take 365.25 days to orbit the sun. In fact, early in its history, it spun around much faster. This meant that days were shorter, so there were more of them in a year. Then, a few million years after it formed, the earth was hit by an object as big as a small planet, causing huge amounts of rock to fly out into space. This rock soon collected together to form the moon, and ever since, the moon's gravity has been slowing down the rotation of the earth. Before the moon was formed, an earth day was just 6 hours long. If the moon had never come into existence, a single day would be 8 hours long, and there would be 1,095 days in a year.

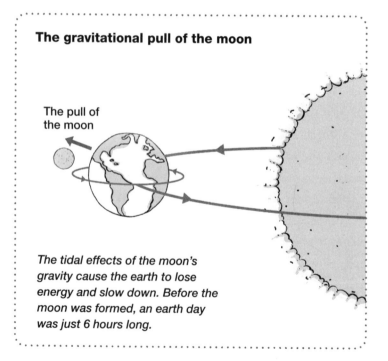

The gravitational pull of the moon

The pull of the moon

The tidal effects of the moon's gravity cause the earth to lose energy and slow down. Before the moon was formed, an earth day was just 6 hours long.

But even though a year may not be as round a quantity as we'd like to think, at least we still have the tidy 24-hour day, right? Not really. First, the rotation of the earth is still slowing down by about half a second per century. Second, the time it takes the earth to spin right around on its axis is actually 23 hours, 56 minutes, and 4 seconds. However, during this time, the earth has moved not just on its axis but also across space, so to spin around to the point where the sun is back in the same place in the sky takes another 3 minutes and 56 seconds, adding up to a grand total of 24 hours.

Why does water freeze?

Water freezes because water molecules stick to one another when they get cold, causing them to slow down.

Water is strange stuff; in fact, it is one of the strangest substances in the known universe. Its odd properties are essential for the evolution and survival of life on Earth, particularly given its ability to form a weak connection called a hydrogen bond, or H-bond.

A sticky business

In liquid form, the individual water molecules are quite energetic, forming and breaking hydrogen bonds with one another at great speed. In other words, they are sticky enough to adhere as a liquid (not flying off, the way molecules in a gas would) but not sticky enough to stay put. When water cools, its molecules lose energy and slow down, and their H-bonds remain stuck together in frozen form.

A water molecule is made up of an oxygen atom connected to two hydrogen atoms, and the way that these atoms share their electrons turns the water molecule into a sort of mini-magnet. Just as two magnets will stick to each other, so a water molecule will stick to other water molecules with H-bonds.

Soon, each water molecule is attached to four others in a rigid lattice or network, forming an ice crystal. The lattice itself is chaotic and very complex. An average ice cube contains about 60 billion trillion molecules. If you had spent every week since the Big Bang coming up with a different arrangement of these molecules, you would not have exhausted the number of possible arrangements! Every single ice cube ever created has probably had its own unique arrangement of water molecules.

Almost any substance will "freeze" if cooled down enough. But why does water freeze so easily? If it weren't for the H-bonds, water would boil at 130°F, and there would be almost no liquid water—and no life—on Earth.

Why do tides ebb and flow?

Tides ebb and flow because the tidal pull of the moon remains stationary while the earth continues to spin around.

Imagine you are on a merry-go-round. It spins on a patch of ground that is flat, aside from a single big bump. Every time your part of the merry-go-round passes over the bump, you rise up in the air. Now, imagine that the merry-go-round is walled in. You can't see out and you don't realize that you are actually going around; because everything you see is moving at the same speed, it feels as if you are the one who's stationary. All you know is that every 30 seconds, the ground rises up. This is the kind of effect experienced by someone sitting at the beach watching the ebb and flow of the tide. It seems like the water is moving while the beach is stationary, but in fact, the beach is moving along with the rest of the earth's surface, and it is the "bump" that is stationary. In this instance, the "bump" is the tidal pull of the moon.

Tides are caused by the gravitational attraction between the moon and the earth. The ground is too solid to move very much in response to the moon's tidal pull, but the oceans are liquid, so they get pulled easily toward it. The result is that the oceans bulge out toward the moon.

While the moon rotates around the earth, it moves pretty slowly compared to the daily rotation of the earth, so for all intents and purposes, the moon stays in the same place as the earth spins around. This means that the tidal bulge caused by the moon also remains inert. That beach you are sitting on passes through the bulge once every 24 hours, and there is also a complementary bulge on the other side of the planet from the moon, so your beach actually passes through two bulges every 24 hours, which is why there are two tides a day. As your beach passes into the bulge, the sea level starts to rise—this is the tide coming in or flowing—until it reaches a maximum height: high tide. Then, as the beach passes out of the bulge, the tide ebbs, or goes out. Some shorelines actually experience two high tides and two low tides a day, two uneven tides a day, or one high and one low tide

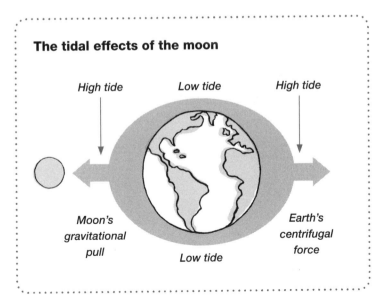

The tidal effects of the moon

High tide   Low tide   High tide

Moon's gravitational pull

Earth's centrifugal force

Low tide

a day. This is determined by the alignment of the sun and moon, as well as the shape of the coastline.

In addition, tides are affected by the gravitational force of the sun and by the depth of the ocean and the shape of the land. At the Bay of Fundy in Nova Scotia, the shape of the coastline and sea bottom combine to create the world's biggest tidal range (or the difference between high and low tide), up to about 56 feet, the height of a five-story building.

Why do things burn?

Things burn because by combining with oxygen, they can move to a lower (and more desirable and stable) energy state.

Burning, technically known as combustion, is a chemical reaction in which a substance combines with oxygen and releases energy in the form of heat and light, which we see as flames. The substance starts off in a higher energy state and, by combining with oxygen, ends up in a lower energy state. In terms of its energy state, matter is like water—it flows downhill. Wherever possible, substances move from a higher to a lower and more stable energy state.

The simplest example of a combustive reaction is when hydrogen burns in oxygen. The two gases combine to produce water, and water is much more stable (that is, harder to move from its current state) than either oxygen or hydrogen—just try setting fire to it and see for yourself. By contrast, both hydrogen and oxygen are highly flammable gases because they exist at much higher energy states than water. The difference between the before and after energy states is the amount of energy that

Catching fire

If burning moves a substance from a higher to a lower energy state, why doesn't combustible stuff like wood burst into flames spontaneously? In fact, it is quite hard to set fire to wood, as anyone who has tried to get a campfire going in the rain will tell you. Some substances will catch fire spontaneously, but they tend not to hang around in the environment all that long. Most require a burst of energy to get the combustive reaction going. This is known as activation energy.

is released during the combustive reaction. A lot of energy is released when hydrogen burns in oxygen, and this makes it a good rocket fuel. The Saturn V rockets that blasted the Apollo moon-landing missions into space used hydrogen and oxygen as fuel—over 960,000 gallons of it! The first-stage tank alone contained enough liquid oxygen to fill 54 railroad tank cars.

The changing energy states of burning wood are like water moving from the top of a slope to the bottom; activation energy is the hump that water has to get over before it can run downhill. Once it gets a little boost to get over the hump, it will continue running downhill until it reaches flat ground. Similarly, once the wood gets a boost from a lit match, it will burn effortlessly. In energetic terms, ash is the equivalent of flat ground. In fact, with wood the picture is more complex, because wood itself doesn't burn directly; instead, once it reaches ignition temperature at about 500°F, the heat causes it to break up and some of it turns into a gas. It is this gas, rather than the wood itself, that burns—but eventually you still wind up with a pile of ashes.

Why does iron rust?

Iron rusts because it combines with oxygen when water is around, forming a new substance called iron oxide, or rust.

Iron is easily converted into iron oxide for the same reason that wood burns: By combining with oxygen, it achieves a lower and more stable energy state. In fact, rusting can be described as a form of combustion, or a very slow form of burning.

Another way to look at rusting is by examining the electrolysis reaction, such as the one that takes place in batteries. An electrolysis reaction is a process involving electricity and chemicals. Electricity is the movement of electrons (subatomic particles with negative charges), and in electrolysis, the electrons come from a piece of metal called an anode. The anode combines with oxygen and releases an electron, which travels through a fluid called an electrolyte. In rusting, you can view the anode as being analogous to the piece of iron, while the electrolyte is water. If the water contains salt, it acts as an even better electrolyte, which is why salt speeds up rusting. This is why objects rust more quickly when exposed to seawater. But salt isn't necessary—even pure water will dissolve carbon dioxide from the air to create a weak acid, and this acts as the electrolyte.

Lady Liberty

Other metals also form oxides, but they are not called rust. Copper forms a layer of oxide known as a patina. One important difference between patina and rust is that patina protects the metal underneath. The skin of the Statue of Liberty is made of copper, and the patina that formed on it has protected it from corrosion so effectively that when the Statue was restored after 100 years of exposure to rain and salt spray, the only part of it that didn't need replacing was the skin. In all that time, the patina had grown to just 0.05 inches thick. Rust, on the other hand, does not protect underlying iron, so a piece of iron will eventually turn completely into iron oxide and crumble away entirely.

Steel is iron that has been strengthened by adding tiny amounts of carbon, but like iron, it is capable of rusting. Stainless steel is a rustproof steel alloy that is made by adding nickel and chromium, which bind to the iron atoms so that they can't bind with oxygen. Another way to protect steel is by covering it with a rustproof coating. Scotland's Forth Bridge, one of the world's largest steel structures, has 478,396 square yards of surface that has to be protected from corrosion, so it is "painted" with a layer of zinc and another of glass flakes.

Why do trees drop their leaves?

Trees drop their leaves when it gets too dry, cold, or dark for them to photosynthesize, at which point it's not worth keeping them around.

Keep in mind that not all trees drop their leaves. Trees that don't drop their leaves are called evergreens. Trees that drop all their leaves at once are called deciduous (from the Latin for "falling down"). Some evergreens, such as trees in tropical rain forests, eventually drop their leaves, but not all at once.

Keeping a leaf alive costs energy. But so does letting one fall, since whatever nutrients are left in the leaf when it falls will be lost to the tree. A tree drops a leaf when it will cost more to keep it alive than to let it fall. This is a bit like having a car; usually, it will be cheaper to keep repairing the car you have rather than buy a new one. But when the car gets old and worn down, it may be a more cost-efficient alternative to scrap it altogether and get a new one.

During dry seasons or cold, dark winters, the cost of keeping a leaf alive goes up, while the amount of photosynthesis it can undergo decreases. Photosynthesis depends on water and light, and as the temperature drops, so does the rate of photosynthesis. For many trees living in the north or south, by the time autumn arrives, it is simply not worth holding on to their leaves. This is especially true for broadleaf trees, which have big, fragile leaves that can be damaged by frost. So deciduous trees decide to cut and run, or, in other words, drop all their leaves at once. A full-grown tree can have more than 200,000 leaves, and over the course of about 60 years, will drop over 1.65 tons of leaves. Worldwide, there are more than 400 billion trees (about 60 for every human being on the planet), so that adds up to a lot of leaves.

When a tree decides that it will be cheaper in the long run to do away with one of its leaves, it drains as many nutrients as possible from the leaf before cutting it off at the base. The order

*A tree drops a leaf when it will cost
more to keep it alive than to let it fall.*

in which these nutrients are drained is the process that causes leaves to change color. Leaves are green because they have a lot of chlorophyll to help them harvest blue and red light, but they also have other types of pigment to help them harvest other colors of light. These pigments include xanthophylls (which are yellow) and carotenoids (which are yellow, orange, and red). Because chlorophyll is the most valuable of these pigments, it gets drained out of the leaf first, leaving the other colors behind, which makes the leaves red, orange, and yellow. Eventually even these colors are drained, leaving only tannins, which are brown.

Why do plants flower in the spring?

Many plants flower in the spring so that they can take advantage of the good weather to reproduce and still have time in the summer to make seeds.

Not all plants flower in the spring. At any given time of year, there will be some flowers in bloom. But spring is the most popular time, because plants that flower then tend to receive a better balance of resources for their different needs.

The plant's ultimate aim is to reproduce, but for this to happen, it must go through a series of steps: fertilization (which is where the flower comes in), seed production, and seed dispersal (which means spreading the seeds to places where they can grow). These jobs are much easier when conditions are good—in other words, when there is plenty of sunlight and water, the temperature is high, and the weather isn't too erratic. In the temperate regions of the world (such as Europe, most of North America, Japan, Argentina, and most of Russia and China), the best weather is in summer, and plants time their activities to take advantage of the season.

If a plant tries to flower in winter, it will struggle to build enough energy for that purpose (which is clearly an energy-intensive endeavor); there won't be many insects around to help pollinate the flower (see below); and bad weather, such as high winds, rain, and frost, will damage or destroy the delicate flower. If a plant waits until summer, it will have much more energy available for flowering, but it may not leave itself enough time to grow seeds and spread them around before winter arrives again. It seems like the best time for most plants to flower is spring: The weather is becoming more temperate, there is ample sunlight to provide energy, and there are plenty of insects around for the business of pollination. The plant then has the whole summer to take advantage of good conditions to grow a healthy, successful seed.

Matchmaking

Plants use flowers to attract insects because they need help with pollination. Pollination is the plant equivalent of sexual reproduction, in which male and female gametes merge to achieve fertilization. Because plants (which are mostly hermaphroditic, meaning they contain the equivalent of both female and male sex organs) can't pick up and wander around looking for a mate, they rely on insects for fertilization. The insect is lured in by the flower, lands on it, and picks up pollen, which it then carries off to fertilize a different flower. Some plants are capable of self-pollination, but this can actually decrease the vigor and viability of the plant, and limit the diversity of its progeny. However, self-pollinating plants can flourish in environments where pollinators are not readily available or exist in small numbers.

Flowers may offer special treats to attract the insects, such as nectar. Honeybees collect nectar from flowers and take it back to their hives to convert into honey, which they consume during the winter when there are no flowers available. It takes a large quantity of nectar to make honey; for just a single pound of honey, bees have to fly about 55,000 miles and tap two million flowers. But the labor is well worth it; an ounce of honey contains enough energy for a bee to fly around the world.

You might be wondering, how do plants know when it's the right time to flower? Some plants seem to measure the temperature before flowering; others rely on the number of hours of daylight. Many species of plants need a cold shock before they will flower, such as the winter frost. There is some evidence that climate change is actually changing the timing of flowering for many plants. According to a study in the journal *Science*, the average first flowering date of 385 British plant species has advanced by 4.5 days over the last 10 years, and one in seven species is flowering more than 2 weeks earlier than usual.

Why did the dinosaurs die out?

The dinosaurs probably died out because of a combination of natural disasters: global warming over millions of years, followed by a series of colossal volcanic eruptions that released vast quantities of poisonous gas, at almost the same time as a massive asteroid smashed into the earth.

The dinosaurs ruled the planet for over 160 million years, but 65 million years ago, something terrible happened that wiped out every species of dinosaur (except for the ancestors of birds). So what was this terrible event? The common explanation these days is that an asteroid or meteorite killed the dinosaurs (an asteroid is bigger than a meteorite, and a meteorite is a meteoroid that has entered a planet's atmosphere), and there is a lot of evidence that an asteroid around 6 miles across slammed into Mexico about 65 million years ago. The crater it left is hidden under rocks and water, beneath an area called Chicxulub, and the event is known as the Chicxulub impact.

The Chicxulub impact blasted a crater more than 100 miles wide, setting off earthquakes around the planet. The explosion took out

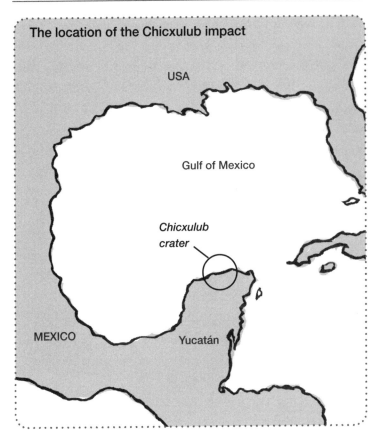

The location of the Chicxulub impact

USA

Gulf of Mexico

Chicxulub crater

MEXICO

Yucatán

most of North America almost instantly with a flash of intense heat and a destructive shock wave, battering the rest of the planet with super-powered hurricanes, or hypercanes, five times more powerful than the biggest hurricanes we get today. A huge wall of water known as a tsunami raced outward from the impact site, reaching up to more than 300 yards high and sweeping nearly 200 miles inland. But all this was only the beginning.

Vast amounts of melted rock were thrown into the sky and rained down all over the planet, setting fire to everything. Up to a quarter of all life on land was burned to ash. The dust and smoke shut out all sunlight, probably for several years, so that the earth froze in the darkness as temperatures fell by up to 59°F. Plants could not photosynthesize, and poisonous gas made the oceans toxic. The ozone layer was damaged, so that when the smoke finally cleared, the earth's surface was bathed in deadly ultraviolet light.

As if this were not bad enough, life on Earth was probably already suffering as the result of a series of volcanic eruptions in an area of what is now India called the Deccan Traps. These were not like ordinary volcanic eruptions; they were much, much worse. About 123,000 cubic miles of molten rock poured out of a titanic gash in the earth's surface. When it cooled, it left a layer of solid rock over 1.24 miles thick in places, covering an area of about 193,000 square miles.

The final blow

The heat, ash, and poisonous gas released by the Deccan Traps eruptions helped push the dinosaurs close to extinction. The Chicxulub impact, contrary to popular belief, was probably the thing that finished them off.

Humanity could easily go the way of the dinosaurs. There are several places on Earth, such as Yellowstone National Park and the area around Naples in Italy, where eruptions on the scale of what occurred in the Deccan Traps could happen at any moment. Also, there are millions of asteroids that cross the earth's orbit, and some of them could be 6 miles wide or bigger. Over a long time scale, your chances of dying because of an asteroid impact are roughly equivalent to your chances of dying in an airplane crash.

Why are we running out of oil?

We are running out of oil because we use it up millions of times faster than it can form.

Oil is formed when tiny plants and animals in the sea die, sink to the bottom of the ocean, get buried under layers of rock, and are crushed and heated until they break down into very simple molecules. This process takes from thousands to even millions of years. So, for all intents and purposes, oil is a nonrenewable resource. This means there is only so much in the ground, and once we suck it out and use it, it is gone.

If you keep using a nonrenewable resource, eventually you will run out because nature is not making any more of it. How soon you will run out depends on how quickly you are using the resource, and as far as oil goes, we are using it very quickly indeed. Global oil consumption hit 87.4 million barrels per day in 2010. This means the world burns through over 1,000 barrels of oil per second.

According to the annual *Statistical Review of World Energy*, produced by oil giant BP, the world's oil reserves at the end of 2010 were estimated to be 1.383 trillion barrels. This means that if oil use continues at the same rate as in 2010, the world will run out of oil in just over 40 years. In fact, the rate of oil consumption continues to rise every year, so the global oil reserve, as estimated by BP, should be depleted even sooner than this. (Incidentally, BP was named by *Multinational Monitor* as one of the 10 worst corporations in both 2001 and 2005, on the basis of its environmental record. In April 2010, one of its drilling rigs exploded, resulting in the largest accidental marine oil spill in the history of the petroleum industry and causing widespread damage to wildlife habitats and human health.)

But the picture is not that simple. On the one hand, there are many who argue that the estimates of how much oil is left are far too optimistic, with oil-producing countries such as Saudi Arabia claiming to have far larger reserves than they actually do. On the other hand, there are many others who argue that we are underestimating oil reserves, as it will be possible to find or produce new types of oil.

An example is the development of oil sands as a source of oil. Oil sand is black and sticky with tar; washing off the tar, collecting it, and refining it make it possible to extract oil. Because this is difficult and expensive, oil sands were not previously considered to be a realistic source of oil, but now conditions have changed— that is, the price of oil has increased, making alternative resources more plausible solutions. Canada is now considered to have the third-largest oil reserves in the world, thanks to the

169 billion barrels of oil that can be extracted from its oil sands. As technology improves, there is a good chance that official estimates of oil reserves will get bigger, so that we may not run out of oil for 50 to 100 years.

Some experts suggest that the question should not be "When will the world run out of oil?" but "When will we need more oil than we can produce?" This moment in history, when demand outstrips supply, is known as the "peak oil" moment, which experts believe will lead to global disaster as oil prices rocket, the world economy collapses, and civilization as we know it is threatened. For instance, over 90 percent of transport in the world depends on oil, so if it suddenly becomes exorbitantly priced, almost no one will be able to afford to fly or drive anywhere.

Why does radioactive material have a half-life?

Radioactive material has a half-life because half-life, as a measurement, is the most sensible way of measuring exponential decay.

Radioactive decay is the process by which a radioactive element, known as a radionuclide, changes into a different radionuclide by shooting out subatomic particles, or energy. The release of subatomic particles or energy is known as radiation.

The half-life of a radionuclide is the length of time it takes for half of the atoms in a sample to decay. For instance, bismuth-212 has a half-life of just over an hour. This means that if you started with 1,000 atoms of bismuth-212, in an hour there would be about 500 atoms left. The others would have decayed to a different radionuclide. After another hour, there would only be around 250 atoms of bismuth-212, and after 3 hours there would be 125.

To simplify, we can use the analogy of flipping a coin to study the principle of a half-life. Imagine that a flipped coin that comes up tails is like a radioactive atom that has decayed, and then imagine you have 1,000 coins; once an hour you flip them all and then throw away the ones that turned up tails. After 1 hour you would have roughly 500 coins, after 2 hours you would have 250, and 3 three hours you would have 125.

Why not just have a number that tells you how long it will take for a radioactive atom to decay? Such a number might be called the lifespan of a radionuclide. The reason that we use half-life instead of lifespan is that radioactive decay is a completely random process. It is controlled by something called the uncertainty principle, which means that it is impossible to say for certain exactly when a radioactive atom will decay. It is only possible to state the probability of that decay, just as it is only possible to state the overall probability of a coin toss coming up heads or tails after flipping it many times.

For an individual atom of bismuth-212, it is possible to say that over the course of an hour there is a 50 percent probability that it will decay, but there is no length of time over which it is possible to say with 100 percent certainty when it will decay. Although it is astronomically unlikely, it is possible that any single atom of bismuth-212 still won't have decayed in 1,000 years.

Bismuth-212 has a relatively short half-life, but the radio-nuclide with the shortest half-life is helium-5, with a half-life of just 7.6×10^{-22} seconds, which is less than a billion trillionth of a second. The radionuclide with the longest half-life is tellurium-128: 2.2 trillion trillion years.

Knowing the half-life of certain radioisotopes is extremely useful and can allow us to determine the ages of ancient artifacts through carbon dating. Scientists routinely use the half-life of carbon-14 to examine objects up to about 60,000 years old. In looking at how much of the carbon-14 has broken down, scientists can estimate the age of an item. Uranium-238 can be used in a similar way to examine much older substances.

Why does the earth quake?

The earth quakes because the surface of the earth is made up of plates that move and grind against one another. Sometimes they stick in place, however, and then suddenly slip.

Earthquakes are caused by sudden movements of the tectonic plates, giant slabs of rock that make up the outer skin of the planet. In some places, these plates slide past each other—but since they are made of rock, they don't slide smoothly. Instead, they get stuck at some points, until strain and stress build up so much that they come apart abruptly, jumping past each other. When this happens, a lot of energy is released and movement ripples out through the earth. On the surface, these ripples cause earthquakes.

The earth can also quake when hot molten rock rises to the surface in a volcano or when other catastrophic events—such as asteroid impacts—occur.

The tectonic plates float on a layer of partially liquid rock called the mantle. This moves very slowly—about one ten-thousandth the speed of the hour hand on a clock. As a result, the tectonic plates themselves generally move equally slowly. North America and Europe, each inhabiting different tectonic plates, are moving no faster than a fingernail grows.

But the forces involved in moving billions of tons of rock are colossal, and these are magnified when the plates stick and tension builds up. The size of the quake that results when the tension is released depends on how long it has been building. This size, or magnitude, is measured with the Richter scale.

Low-magnitude quakes are amazingly common. A quake of less than magnitude 3.4 happens over 800,000 times a year, but is too small for anyone to notice. Magnitude 4.3 to 4.8 quakes will rattle the houses of a window; they occur nearly 5,000 times a year. It takes a quake of 6.2 or greater to be considered truly dangerous, and 7.4 to collapse most buildings; fortunately, such a large-magnitude quake only happens about 4 times a year.

Great shakes

The Richter scale is a logarithmic scale, which means that each point on it is 10 times greater than the one before. So a magnitude 2 earthquake is 10 times bigger than a magnitude 1 quake, but 100 times smaller than a magnitude 4 quake.

The amount of energy released by a big quake is formidable. The energy released in the San Francisco earthquake of 1906 was comparable to one of the largest nuclear bombs ever created, but the quake was only around 7.8 in magnitude. The biggest quake ever recorded was the southern Chile quake of 1960, which registered 9.5 on the Richter scale. The Tohoku earthquake that caused the devastating tsunami in Japan in March 2011 was 9.0 in magnitude.

Why is the world getting warmer?

The world is getting warmer because of the buildup of greenhouse gases in the atmosphere, which are produced primarily by humans via the burning of forests and fossil fuels.

To illustrate the greenhouse effect, let's think of how a greenhouse works. Essentially, the glass of a greenhouse lets light through but traps heat. Sunlight can get through the glass, and when it hits the inside of the greenhouse, it heats up the space and heat is radiated out. In a more open environment, the heat would simply escape, but in a greenhouse, the glass traps the heat.

The greenhouse effect works similarly on a global scale. On a planet like Mars, with a thin atmosphere, sunlight warms the ground, but that heat can simply escape into space. This is why the surface temperature of Mars varies more widely than Earth's. In contrast, Earth's thick atmosphere—which includes carbon dioxide, water vapor, and other greenhouse gases—allows sunlight in but also retains heat. As a result, the average global temperature on the ground is 59°F. Without the greenhouse effect, the surface temperature would be closer to 0.4°F, and life on the surface wouldn't be viable.

It's getting hot in here

The greenhouse effect is essential to the survival of life on Earth, but over the last century or more, the earth has been warming up. The amount and cause of this climate change is very controversial, but the overwhelming majority of scientists agree that the earth is getting warmer and that industrial pollution by humankind is primarily responsible. This kind of warming is known as anthropogenic, which means "caused by humans."

In the current debate over global warming, there are two main questions:

1. Is global warming real?
2. Is global warming man-made?

The answer to the first question is that temperatures have increased over the last century by about 1.44°F averaged across the globe. Most of this warming has come about in the last 30 years, and the 10 warmest years on record occurred after 1998. Long answer short: According to the numbers, global warming certainly appears to be real.

The answer to the second question is more complicated. It is impossible to determine with 100 percent certainty whether global warming is entirely man-made, because it is not possible to do a controlled experiment comparing our Earth with another Earth where there have been no greenhouse gas emissions from human activity.

At the same time, we know that human activity currently pumps about 7 billion tons of carbon into the atmosphere every year, mostly in the form of carbon dioxide. We also know that natural carbon emissions—from things like the oceans, volcanoes, forest fires, and decaying plants—add up to 150 billion tons a year.

Clearly, the earth is used to dealing with natural emissions, and for many millennia the amount of carbon dioxide in the atmosphere remained constant, at around 280 parts per million (ppm). However, human activity such as industrial farming and fossil-fuel power stations have pumped extra carbon dioxide into the atmosphere, upsetting the long-standing and delicate natural balance.

The National Climatic Data Center announced that 2012 was the hottest year on record since 1895. Temperature differences between years are typically measured in fractions of a degree, but 2012 more than surpassed the previous record set in 1998 by a full degree Fahrenheit. In fact, there were 34,008 new daily record highs set across the country. The carbon dioxide concentrate in the atmosphere is now around 387 ppm, an increase of 38 percent. Two-thirds of this increase has happened in the last 50 years alone. As a result, carbon dioxide levels are now 30 percent higher than at any time over the last 800,000 years.

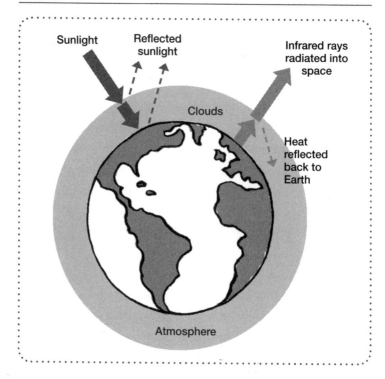

Bottom line: The world is getting warmer, and humans clearly have a powerful, unprecedented influence on the climate. Because the climate takes a long time to respond to changes in greenhouse gas levels, most of the warming resulting from gas emissions in the air today is yet to happen. If we continue to produce carbon dioxide at the current rate, the world could warm up over the next few centuries to temperatures that would make much of the earth uninhabitable.

According to the British Geological Society, it will take the earth 100,000 years to recover from these changes in gas levels. Even if we cut our emissions so that carbon dioxide levels don't ever exceed 560 ppm, the earth could still warm up to about 3°F to 7°F by 2100, according to the Environmental Protection Agency (EPA). The upper limit of this range is more than the difference between the present day and the last Ice Age, while even the lower end of the range would be the biggest temperature change in the entire history of civilization. According to the Intergovernmental Panel on Climate Change (IPCC), this will probably melt so much ice from Antarctica, Greenland, and elsewhere that sea levels will rise anywhere from about 3 to 35 inches by 2100.

Although the boom in natural gas, which is replacing coal at many power stations, has led to lower emissions in some areas of the world, this decline is exceeded by continued growth in developing countries. Coal, which is the most carbon-intensive fossil fuel around, is growing the fastest, and coal-related emissions increased by over 5 percent in 2011. At this rate, according to the Global Carbon Project, the current international goal of limiting the warming of the planet to about 3 degrees is probably not attainable.

Despite the United Nations Framework Convention on Climate Change's attempt to make the countries of the world reach a consensus on global climate change, there are few controls in place to curb man-made emissions—not to mention the fact that many nations disagree on several factors, ranging from the urgency of protecting rain forests to the need for clean-energy technology to the differing obligations of industrialized and developing nations.

Why do volcanoes erupt?

Volcanoes erupt because gas-filled molten rock rises to the earth's surface.

A volcano is a naturally occurring rupture in the earth's surface that is capable of erupting with a combination of hot molten rock, solid rock, ash, and gas. There are about 1,800 active volcanoes in the world, and at least 20 of them are erupting right now. When the molten rock comes out of the ground, it is called lava, but while it is still in the ground, it is called magma. Magma is the reason volcanoes erupt.

The earth has a solid crust around the outside, but that crust is pretty thin compared to the entire planet—only about 6 to 22 miles thick in most places. If the earth were the size of a standard basketball, the crust would only be about 0.016 inches thick.

Underneath the crust is a layer of very hot rock that is not quite liquid but not quite solid, called the mantle. Sometimes a bubble of magma forms in the mantle. Because it is very hot (up to 2,282°F when it comes out of the ground) and full of gas, it is less dense than the rest of the mantle and rises toward the surface. When it gets to the solid crust, it forces its way up through cracks.

So, why does the magma bubble form in the first place? Magma is formed at the boundaries where tectonic plates meet. Tectonic plates are the huge slabs of rock that make up the earth's crust. They move about relative to one another. Some of them move apart, while others ram into each other, forcing the edge of one of the plates to dive down under the other plate. The first type of boundary is called a spreading boundary, and the second is called a subduction zone.

Spreading boundaries release pressure in the hot mantle. As the pressure drops, the hot rock can turn into liquid and become magma. In subduction zones, the subducted crust is plunged deep into the mantle, where extreme heat melts the rock and causes magma to bubble up.

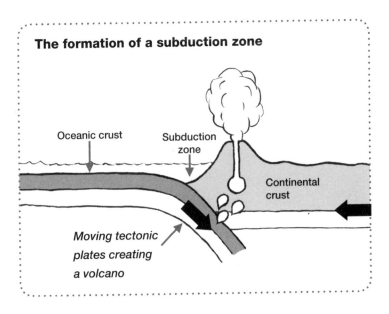

The formation of a subduction zone

Oceanic crust

Subduction zone

Continental crust

Moving tectonic plates creating a volcano

This is why about 94 percent of known eruptions have been restricted to a few belts of volcanic activity, covering less than 0.6 percent of the earth's surface. These belts correspond to plate boundaries. The best known of these belts is the one surrounding the Pacific plate, which is called the Pacific Ring of Fire; it is home to 90 percent of the world's volcanoes.

Why is the sea salty?

The sea is salty because minerals from the earth's crust are dissolved by water and washed or blasted into the sea.

Four cups of seawater contains about 7 teaspoons of salt—that's only a little over an ounce. Only about 2.5 teaspoons of this is table salt (sodium chloride); in fact, there are at least 72 chemical elements dissolved in seawater, which almost certainly contain every naturally occurring element on Earth. There is enough salt in the sea to cover the land to a depth of nearly 500 feet.

Rivers and most lakes are nowhere near as salty as the sea. Seawater is 220 times saltier than fresh lake water. So why are the oceans so salty, while lakes and rivers are not?

In fact, water from lakes and rivers is a bit salty. When rain falls onto the ground, seeps through the soil and rock, and flows over the ground in streams and rivers, it picks up and dissolves minerals. Eventually, these are washed out to sea. Rivers and streams flowing from the United States alone dump about 248 million tons of dissolved solids into the sea every year.

Giving vent

Salt also gets into the ocean from hydrothermal vents—fissures in the earth's surface. So much water blasts out of these vents that if the oceans were drained dry, it would only take 10 million years for the vents to refill them. Once the salt gets into the sea, it is concentrated by evaporation.

With all this salt flowing into the ocean and so much water evaporating, the real question is not why is the ocean salty, but why isn't it getting saltier? If the oceans lost all their salt overnight, it would take about 250 million years for the world's rivers to replenish them, yet the rivers have been emptying salt into the oceans for a lot longer than that.

The saltiness of the sea stays the same because the oceans lose salt at pretty much the same rate as they gain it. Salt is lost when it gets laid down as part of new sedimentary rock at the bottom of the sea, and it is filtered out when seawater seeps down into the crust of the earth through cracks in the sea floor.

Why is the ground solid?

The ground is solid because it is made up of atoms with electrons that cannot be squeezed any closer to the nuclei they orbit.

In 1911, the New Zealand physicist Ernest Rutherford (1871–1937) shot subatomic particles at a piece of gold film. Some of the particles passed right through, but some bounced straight back. Rutherford realized that the atom was not a big solid mass, as had previously been thought. Further research revealed that the atom is like a tiny solar system, with almost all of its mass concentrated into a minute nucleus in the center, which is orbited by still more minute electrons. Most startlingly of all, there is nothing in between these particles: 99.999999999999 percent of the volume of an atom is just empty space!

If you are sitting in a chair or standing on a floor while you read this, think about what is holding you up. Less than one part in 100,000 of that solid surface is actually made of something. The rest is just empty space. This means that humans also consist of primarily empty space if we look at our composition on an atomic level.

So, if both you and the floor are mostly empty space, what stops you from falling straight through the floor?

The reason that solids are solid is that electrons have to obey two laws of quantum physics known as the Pauli exclusion principle and the Heisenberg uncertainty principle. The first law says that two electrons cannot occupy the same place. The second principle says that you can know either the location or the speed of an electron, but not both at the same time.

The uncertainty principle means that the more you pin down the location of an electron by confining the space it can occupy, the greater the possible range of speeds it can travel. The electron is like an angry bee in a shrinking box—the more the box shrinks, the more frantically it buzzes about. If you try to squeeze the electron any closer to the nucleus, its energy levels go through the roof.

To squeeze a solid into a smaller space by just 1 percent would raise the energy of the electrons in it by the same amount as heating them by more than 1,800°F. This is why you cannot crush a solid into a smaller volume and, hence, why solids are solid and you don't fall through the floor.

Why does it rain?

It rains because warm air can hold more water than cool air; when wet air cools down, it can no longer hold as much water, so the water condenses and falls to the earth as rain, snow, or hail.

Temperatures fall as altitude increases, so warm, wet air cools down as it rises. Warm air is less dense than cool air, so warm air will tend to rise on its own. It can also be forced upward by terrain or by another air mass. Each of these scenarios leads to a different type of rain.

When water evaporates from a puddle of water, some of the water molecules in the puddle will be moving about as fast as if they were at boiling point, and some of these will escape from the puddle and into the air as water vapor. The air can only hold so much of this water vapor; once it reaches its limit, the extra water will condense into visible droplets, forming clouds or fog, and some of these droplets will fall as precipitation or rain.

The amount of vapor the air can hold depends on temperature. Warmer air can hold more vapor, but because it is not as dense as cool air, it will tend to rise. The atmosphere cools by about 44°F for every 3,000 feet you rise. As the warm, wet air rises, it also cools demonstrably, and above a certain point, water vapor condenses into droplets.

Not all rains are exactly the same

Convective rain falls when pockets of warm, wet air rise because they are less dense than the surrounding, cooler air. This occurs when the ground is heated by direct sunlight on a warm day. Warm, wet air can also be forced up as it passes over mountains, causing orographic rain, or it can be forced up when it runs into a mass of cold air. The warm and cold air masses don't mix; instead, the warmer one is forced up and over the denser, colder air, creating a weather front, which leads to frontal rain. A typical weather front consists of a billion tons of warm air overlaying more than 800 million tons of colder air.

The clouds that form as a result can be enormous: A typical cumulus cloud (the individual fluffy cloud that might be seen floating around on a mostly sunny day) weighs just over 1.1 million pounds, equivalent to about 100 elephants. That's enough water to fill 7 average-sized backyard swimming pools. A storm cloud, on the other hand, can hold over a million *tons* of water.

Compared to the water in the oceans and ice caps, and even to the water in rivers and lakes, the amount of water in the atmosphere is relatively small—if the water in the atmosphere fell as rain all at once, the oceans would only get around an inch deeper. But try telling that to the people who live in Mawsynram, India, probably the wettest place in the world, where the average annual rainfall is about 468 inches, or to the inhabitants of Waialeale in Hawaii, which has an average of 335 rainy days a year. They probably long to visit Arica, Chile, which boasts 1 day of rain every 6 years.

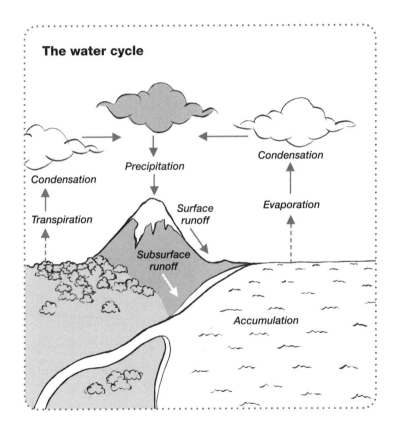

The water cycle

THE
HUMAN
BODY
AND MIND

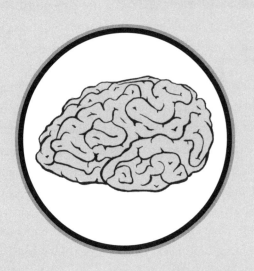

Why can't we hear dog whistles?

We can't hear dog whistles because they are too high pitched for human ears.

Humans can hear a limited range of pitch or frequencies. Sound that is too high pitched or too high frequency for us to hear is known as ultrasound, whereas sound that is too low pitched is called infrasound. The pitch or frequency of a sound is measured in hertz (Hz), or vibrations per second; 1 Hz = one vibration per second. A thousand vibrations per second is called a kilohertz, or kHz. Most people hear sounds within the range 20 Hz–20 kHz, although younger people have a wider range of hearing than older people, and women have a wider range than men.

Dogs can hear much higher pitches than we can, so they can hear dog whistles, which make sounds in the 20–22 kHz range. Dog whistles let dog trainers and owners make a loud noise that the dog can hear from a distance but that won't bother other humans. But the whistle itself has no special power to command the dog; an animal will only respond if it's been trained to do so.

Other animals that can hear ultrasound include bats and dolphins, which use ultrasonic clicks and whistles for echolocation (the animal version of sonar). By sending out sounds and measuring how long they take to bounce back, these animals can "see" with sound.

There are lots of animals that use infrasound, too. Giraffes are usually thought of as silent creatures, but in fact, they are quite garrulous with the use of infrasound. Many other large animals use infrasound; tigers use it to stun their prey, and the infrasonic booms of elephants can be heard by other elephants over 6 miles away. Blue whales make such loud infrasonic noises that a human swimming next to the whale's throat would have his brain turned to jelly! Natural forces like earthquakes and tsunamis generate infrasound, and it is believed that animals are able to avoid being swept away by tsunamis because they pick up infrasonic warnings and flee well before the wave hits.

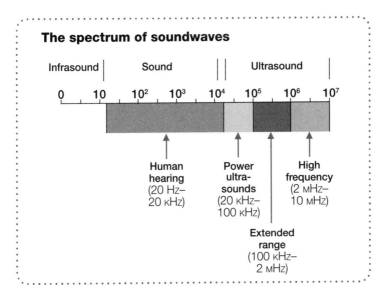

The spectrum of soundwaves

Infrasound | Sound | | | Ultrasound |

0   10 10^2 10^3 10^4 10^5 10^6 10^7

Human hearing (20 Hz– 20 kHz)

Power ultra- sounds (20 kHz– 100 kHz)

High frequency (2 mHz– 10 mHz)

Extended range (100 kHz– 2 mHz)

So, why can't humans hear infrasound and ultrasound? The answer is probably linked to the size of the human body and what we use sound for. Big animals like elephants and tigers need a lot of food, so they can't afford to have too many individuals living close together or they would quickly run out of things to eat. But they still need to communicate to find mates and warn off enemies, so they use infrasound because it can be heard a long way away. Being big makes it easier for them to generate loud, low-frequency noise.

For small animals, it is easier to make high-pitched noises, which suit their needs better, as they are useful for bursts of communication across short distances. In terms of size, humans are in between, and we need to hear sounds such as other people's voices, so the most useful frequency range for us is about 20 Hz–20 kHz. Evolution favors individuals who make the most efficient use of their resources, and growing a hearing system that can accommodate both infrasound and ultrasound would be very expensive in terms of material and energy. The most efficient solution is to grow ears that only hear the most useful range of frequencies, and this is exactly what has happened.

Why is blood red?

Blood is red because it contains iron.

Red blood cells contain iron, which can be found in a protein called hemoglobin. These doughnut-shaped cells float in a fluid known as plasma that flows through the veins and arteries in your body.

Plasma itself is pale yellow, but suspended in it are billions of red blood cells, about 5 million per milliliter of blood. There are about 12 pints of blood in your body, making up around 7 percent of your total weight. Your heart pumps this blood around your body at a tremendous rate; an average red blood cell circulates through the body three times a minute, traveling 12,000 miles a day—the equivalent of traveling from California to New York and back twice!

Not all blood is red; horseshoe crabs and some other animals have blue blood, while insects may have green blood (although it isn't technically blood—more about this in just a bit). Horseshoe crab blood is blue because, instead of hemoglobin, it has a related protein called hemocyanin, which contains copper instead of iron. In its deoxygenated form, hemocyanin is colorless, making

Blue on the outside

It is a common misconception that since veins look blue beneath the skin, they must contain blue blood. It is true that veins carry deoxygenated blood (blood that has given up most of its oxygen and is traveling back to the lungs to pick up some more), and that this is a slightly different color from the oxygenated blood found in the arteries. However, the veins look blue because the only color of light that can penetrate the skin, bounce off the outside of the vein, and travel back through the skin to your eyes is blue. Deoxygenated blood is actually a dark purplish red, while oxygenated blood is bright red. Dark blood exposed to the air will quickly turn bright red as it absorbs oxygen.

the crab's blood a pale grayish color; however, when copper is bound to oxygen, it turns blue, giving the horseshoe crab blood a startling blue color.

Insect "blood" is not used for oxygen transport at all, so it shouldn't really be called blood; the correct term is *hemolymph*. So if insects don't use blood to carry oxygen, how do their cells get the oxygen they need? Insects have evolved a more direct route for oxygen transport—a system of air passages that reach into every nook and cranny, so that no cell is far from a direct source of oxygen. This tends to place a ceiling on the maximum possible size that insects can reach, which is why mammals can be as large as blue whales but insects no bigger than a hand-sized cockroach. Insects use their hemolymph to carry food, and it can either be colorless or it can pick up color from what the insects eat—which is why vegetarian insects sometimes have green blood.

Why do we get old?

The most common understanding of why we get old is that our bodies' repair mechanisms stop working as well as they did when we were younger.

Actually, this is more of a description of *how* we get old. Nobody really knows *why* we get old. In fact, not all animals age, so it may be possible for humans to avoid this fate as well someday.

Various theories in biology concern aging. Some people think that our bodies can soak up only so much damage, such as cell damage and environmental stresses, before the repair mechanisms that mend this damage are exhausted and stop working. Another theory concerns the ways our cells avoid turning into cancer cells: It may be that the same mechanism that helps a young person avoid getting cancer (making cells kill themselves before they become dangerous) eventually causes the same person to get old. This is called the antagonistic pleiotropy theory. A third theory, called the disposable soma theory, suggests that our bodies exist only to push our reproductive cells into the next generation. It doesn't matter if the messenger (or, in biological jargon, the soma) gets damaged or killed, as long as he or she delivers the message before dying. In other words, our reproductive cells are important, but we are disposable.

The aforementioned theories paint a bleak picture, as they suggest that aging has no ultimate purpose, and that we get old because it is impossible not to get old. But some animals don't seem to get old. The Aldabra giant tortoise can live to at least 255 years, and no one knows how much longer it might survive without any external threats. The same is true of the rougheye rockfish (its oldest known specimen lived up to 205 years), and even the humble lobster. The quahog clam is another trouper—it can live for over 400 years! The oldest animal ever discovered is a quahog clam nicknamed Ming, which was over 405 years old when it was fished out of the ocean near Iceland.

Aldabra giant tortoise

To take into account the ability of some animals to apparently live without aging, some biologists have suggested that human aging does have a function, and that we have actually evolved to grow old. Age and death might help clear the way for our descendants to be more genetically successful, or it might be that aging poses such a survival challenge that it acts as a kind of test, weeding out weaker individuals so that only the strongest survive.

If we really have evolved to grow old, then the aging process must be under the control of our genes, which in turn means we can do something about it. Advances in genetic science and the ability to modify our genes through genetic engineering might make it possible for future humans to stay young forever—or at least to reverse the visible effects of aging.

Why do we feel pain?

Our brain enables us to recognize (or feel) pain so that we will stop doing whatever is causing the pain—which thus aids our overall chances of survival.

Pain is your body's way of informing your brain that your body is being damaged. If something causes damage to the cells of, say, your foot, pain receptors in your foot fire off signals that travel along your nerves to your brain. Your brain translates these signals into the sensation of pain, which enables you to do what you can to stop the pain. For example, if you experience pain after stepping on a very pointy rock, you'll most likely remove your foot from it. Without pain, you wouldn't know that you needed to move your foot, and so you might end up losing it, which wouldn't make your odds of survival particularly favorable.

In fact, people who cannot feel pain don't live very long. There are some conditions, such as syringomyelia, which stop the pain receptors from working properly, and as a result, people don't feel pain. This can be dangerous in lots of ways; keeping in mind the above example, if you don't realize you've cut your foot, you won't do anything to stop it from getting infected. But the greatest danger to people who can't feel pain is joint damage. If you hold one position for too long, your joints will start to hurt, prompting you to change position before you've done any damage to your joints. People with syringomyelia wouldn't be prompted to change their position because they wouldn't realize they are damaging their joints, which ends up destroying them. Eventually, they can die of blood poisoning.

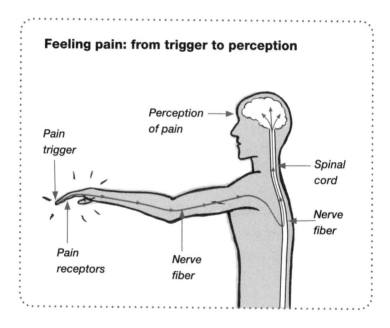

Feeling pain: from trigger to perception

Perception of pain

Pain trigger

Spinal cord

Nerve fiber

Pain receptors

Nerve fiber

Pain can be a difficult sensation to describe, because everyone's experience of it is different. Dr. Justin Schmidt studies biting and stinging insects, and he has devised a fairly descriptive scale that rates and describes the pain caused by these different bugs. At the bottom of the scale, with a pain rating of 1.0, is the sweat bee; Schmidt describes its sting as "light . . . almost fruity . . . [as if] a tiny spark has singed a single hair on your arm." Near the middle of the scale comes the bullhorn acacia ant, with a score of 1.8; its bite feels like "someone has fired a staple into your cheek." The most painful insect is the pepsis wasp—its sting scores 4.0, and Schmidt describes the sensation as akin to "a running hair dryer [that] has been dropped into your bubble bath."

Why do we sleep?

We sleep to recharge our energy and give our brains breathing room so they can rewire themselves.

At least, this is the dominant theory right now. It used to be thought that there was no special reason for sleep, and that it was just what happened when animals stopped moving to save energy and stay out of trouble. But we now know that all animals sleep, even those that live in the sea and must keep moving to survive. We also know that animals that don't get enough sleep suffer and eventually die, so there must be a purpose and function behind sleep. We simply don't know exactly what it is yet.

Wear and tear

There are many different theories for why we need to sleep. Animals that are not allowed to sleep get sick and die: Their wounds don't heal, they lose weight, their skin gets bad and their immune systems break down. So one reason we need to sleep is probably so that the body can repair and look after itself in a way that it can't while awake.

The longest a human being has gone without sleep is 11 days (264 hours). People who go for so long without sleep experience hallucinations and memory loss; become paranoid, confused, and ill tempered; and cannot do simple tasks such as adding or counting. Not getting enough sleep over a long period interferes with memory and inhibits people from learning. But it isn't true that sleeping is a completely restful pastime. Researchers have discovered that sleeping brains experience bursts of activity. This has led scientists to theorize that one function of sleep is to give the brain a chance to reorganize itself, file away all the information picked up during the day, and complete tasks that it can't do while awake.

The sleepiest animal in the world may be the koala, which sleeps about 22 hours a day. Male lions supposedly sleep for up to 20 hours a day, leaving female lions to do the "lion's share" of the work! Arguably the least sleepy animal is the dolphin, because it always keeps one side of its brain awake (and one eye open), probably because it would drown otherwise.

Why do we have 46 chromosomes?

Humans have 46 chromosomes because the great apes, with whom we share common ancestors, have 24 pairs of chromosomes; and some time after humans split from the great apes, two of these chromosomes merged.

Humans have two copies of 23 chromosomes, giving us a grand total of 46. Great apes, such as chimpanzees and gorillas, have two sets of 24 chromosomes, giving them 48 in total. Around 6 to 8 million years ago, humans and great apes shared an ancestor, an ape with two sets of 24 chromosomes. But after our species split from the apes, two of these 24 chromosomes got stuck together to form the human chromosome 2. Chromosome 2 looks like two chimpanzee chromosomes joined together, because in evolutionary terms, that is exactly what it is.

Chromosome fusing is actually surprisingly common. About 1 in 1,000 babies have two chromosomes stuck together, and it usually makes no difference to their health (although half of their eggs or sperm will be infertile). The same process occurs in other animals. Wild horses have 33 pairs of chromosomes (giving them 66 in total), but domesticated ones have 32 pairs (giving them 64 in total). That means horses have recently undergone the same chromosomal fusing that humans did millions of years ago.

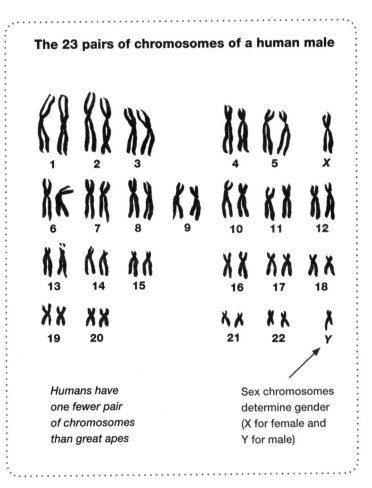

The 23 pairs of chromosomes of a human male

1 2 3 4 5 X

6 7 8 9 10 11 12

13 14 15 16 17 18

19 20 21 22 Y

Humans have one fewer pair of chromosomes than great apes

Sex chromosomes determine gender (X for female and Y for male)

Mr. Potato

Humans have 46 chromosomes because our ape ancestors had 48—but why exactly did they have 48? Nobody knows. In fact, there seems to be no special significance to the number of chromosomes a plant or animal has. We have the same number of chromosomes as the potato. Chickens have 78, a goldfish has 94, and there is a type of fern (Ophioglossum reticulatum) *that has 1,260 chromosomes.*

The exact number of chromosomes an animal or plant has probably comes down to random mistakes. When an animal or plant makes special cells for reproduction (called gametes), it usually splits its sets of chromosomes in half. In humans, each sperm or egg cell gets just one copy of each of the 23 chromosomes. When a sperm and egg come together during fertilization, the fertilized egg has 46 chromosomes. But the chromosome sorting process often goes wrong, and it is easy to end up with a sperm or egg that has two copies of one of the chromosomes, or even all 46 chromosomes. In humans, such gametes cannot usually make a baby, but in some other animals and plants, this doesn't seem to be a major obstacle to reproduction. When you add to this the possibility of chromosomes fusing together, as has happened with humans and horses, you can see that it is easy to end up with any number of chromosomes.

Why do we have X and Y chromosomes?

We have X and Y chromosomes because about 170 million to 310 million years ago, what used to be a second X chromosome lost most of its genes, along with the ability to swap genes with the other X chromosome; it became the Y chromosome.

Many other animals, including the ones we evolved from at about that same time, have two X chromosomes and no Y chromosome, so perhaps a better question would be: Why do some humans have a Y chromosome? The answer is, like most species of animal, we need a way to make both male and female babies, and the Y chromosome is what humans have evolved to achieve this. In humans, whether you are male or female is decided by whether you have a Y chromosome.

We all have 23 pairs of chromosomes, giving us 46 chromosomes in total. Out of these 23 pairs, 22 are identical copies of each other, so that a person has two copies of chromosome 1, two copies of chromosome 2, and so on. The only exception to this is the pair known as the sex chromosomes. These come in two different "flavors," called X and Y, because they look a bit like the letters X and Y when seen under a microscope.

The Y chromosome carries the genes that determine maleness. So if a baby grows from an egg that has one copy of the X chromosome and one Y chromosome, it will turn out to be a boy. If the baby has two X chromosomes and no Y chromosome, it will not have the male genes and will develop into a girl.

The Y chromosome used to be an X, and the earliest mammals all had two X chromosomes. In other words, they didn't have sex chromosomes, which means they must have had a different method of determining which babies would be male and which female, just as fish, birds, and reptiles do today. In some animals, such as alligators and turtles, the temperature of the egg determines its sex; in others, the distribution of hormones does. Some fish, such as the clownfish, can even change sex after they are fully grown to compensate for a lack of males or females.

Why can't we breathe underwater?

We can't breathe underwater because our lungs cannot extract enough of the oxygen that is dissolved in water.

Fish can breathe underwater, so why can't we? Also, why can't fish breathe when they are out of the water? Fish use gills, which are similar to lungs in both form and function. But if gills and lungs are similar, why do we require air to breathe, while fish require water?

The answer is that gills and lungs are each specialized for their particular environments. Seawater contains 1.5 to 2.5 percent dissolved air, and about a third of this is oxygen. This turns out to be sufficient for fish, as they are cold blooded and have low oxygen needs compared to warm-blooded animals with higher metabolic rates, like mammals and birds. Fish evolved gills to help them extract dissolved oxygen from water. Gills have lots of tiny blood vessels very close to the surface of the skin, which is so thin that it is referred to as a membrane. Oxygen from the water can easily pass across the gill membrane into the blood, and waste gases such as carbon dioxide can pass out.

Gills work fine when they are wet, and in fact, a fish could breathe on land if there were some way to keep its gills constantly refreshed with water. When animals left the sea and moved onto land, they couldn't manage this feat, so they needed a different system: lungs. With lungs, the whole process relocates to the body's internal environment, where the lung membranes can be kept wet, protected, and warm. With lungs, land animals have been able to take advantage of the much higher level of oxygen in the atmosphere; at sea level the air is about 21 percent oxygen, offering up to forty times more oxygen than water. Since oxygen is needed to power the muscles, the brain, and the rest of the body, air-breathing animals can be much more active than their water-breathing counterparts. This is why mammals that live in the sea, like whales and dolphins, have kept their lungs and still need to come to the surface to breathe air.

Below the surface

Lungs won't work underwater because getting filled up with water damages the delicate setup inside the lungs. And even if we had gills, we wouldn't be able to breathe underwater, as there simply isn't enough oxygen in the water to meet our needs.

The closest a human can get to the experience of breathing underwater is to breathe perfluorocarbon, a liquid that can dissolve high levels of oxygen. Breathing liquid would make it possible for divers to go much deeper, because they wouldn't have the problems with the pressure generated from breathing compressed air. James Cameron's film *The Abyss* memorably features a character who breathes perfluorocarbon in order to descend to great depths underwater.

Why can't we eat grass?

We can't eat grass because we don't have bacteria in our guts that can break down tough cellulose.

In fact, we do eat grass—lots of it. About three quarters of all the food humankind eats comes from grasses, specifically wheat, rice, and corn. But the bits we eat are the seeds, not the green, leafy stems. Grass stems and similar green leafy bits of plants make up the major part of the diet of many common animals, including cows, sheep, kangaroos, and horses. So if they can eat it, why can't we?

The answer lies in one of the main differences between grass and us. The cells that make up our bodies are relatively flimsy, because they are protected only by a fragile membrane made of a thin layer of fat. The cells that make up plants are much stronger, because in addition to a membrane, they have an extra layer of protection: a cell wall made of a tough, starchy substance known as cellulose. Humans cannot digest cellulose, which is why we can't live off grass. The adhesive tape we use to wrap gifts or fasten paper to walls is made of cellulose, which should give you an idea of how inedible it is.

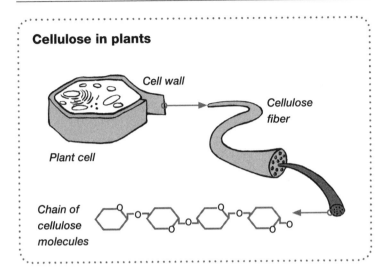

Cellulose in plants

Cell wall

Cellulose fiber

Plant cell

Chain of cellulose molecules

Cellulose is a very long molecule formed by linking many small sugar molecules together. Humans can digest sugar easily enough, so why can't our guts cope with cellulose? In order to break up cellulose and split it into simple sugars, an enzyme called cellulase is needed. Unfortunately, we don't make cellulase.

Cows and other grass-eating animals don't make cellulase either, but they have a lot of tiny friends who do: the bacteria that live in their digestive tracts. These special bacteria live in a symbiotic relationship with the animals, which means that everyone benefits. The bacteria get a nice, warm place to live and a constant supply of chewed-up grass to feed on, and in return, the animal takes advantage of the digestive enzymes that only the bacteria can produce. The bacteria get to work on the tough cellulose in the grass, breaking it up and feeding off some of the sugars, but there are enough left over to keep the animal host happy. Even so, grass-eating animals have to work hard to help their bacterial friends; they have to chew the grass extensively, and many of them have several stomachs so that they can chew, digest, regurgitate, and chew a bit more.

Humans also have a lot of "friendly" bacteria living in their guts—around 100 trillion of them! That means you have at least ten times more bacteria in your intestines than cells in your actual body. But we have never acquired grass-eating bacteria.

Biologists of the future might be able to engineer grass-eating bacteria that will survive in our guts, making it possible for us to digest cellulose. But even then, we probably wouldn't manage to survive on grass. As a defense mechanism to repel grazing animals like rabbits and sheep, grass has evolved a sort of internal armor plating in the form of silica. Silica is the same substance that sand and glass are made of, and it makes the grass very tough—so tough that the teeth of grass-eating animals are continuously ground down. Once their teeth get ground too much, they can't eat any more and end up starving to death. This is what happens to small grass-eating animals like voles, and is probably why horses went extinct in North America about 6 million years ago: The type of grass available changed to one with high silica content, and the horses starved. They only reappeared in the sixteenth century, when Spanish invaders reintroduced them to the continent.

Why do we dream?

Because the brain is such a complex organ, nobody has a conclusive explanation for why we dream.

Dreams are one of the world's enduring mysteries, alongside consciousness and the meaning of life. Because there are numerous categories of dreams, it is challenging to entertain one single theory on their function. They can be bizarre or boring, inconsequential or full of meaning. In ancient times, dreams were believed to be messages from the gods or evidence that the spirit voyages to other worlds during slumber. Only recently have sleep scientists learned enough about dreaming to speculate on whether it has any function and what the function might be.

So what do we know about dreams? Children under the age of 10 don't dream that much, but over the age of 10 you can expect to have at least four dreams a night, varying in length from 5 to 34 minutes. The vast majority of these dreams are not remembered.

Dreams mostly happen during a phase of slumber known as rapid eye movement (REM) sleep, during which your brain and body are aroused in much the same way they are when awake. Although you can also dream in other stages of sleep, REM dreams tend to be the most vivid and memorable.

We also know that although dreams can be about anything, there are some features that tend to be typical. One of the most commonly reported dreams is about being chased or followed. Dreams usually feature the dreamer as him or herself, and most of the other people in the dream will be familiar in some context. Dreams often include bizarre content, in terms of people behaving oddly or objects in the environment transforming suddenly. Dreams tend to be highly emotional, and they primarily feature difficult emotions, such as fear, anxiety, and anger.

Sleep experts have devised a number of theories to explain why we dream and why dreaming evolved in the first place. The psychoanalyst Sigmund Freud posited that dreams help us deal with emotional and psychological problems. A similar theory notes that dreams offer us a way to reflect on our emotions, especially since our brains are working extra hard during the day on everything from mental to physiological functions. The chance to process and understand our emotional landscapes doesn't always occur in the midst of everything that's going on in our internal and external environments, so dreams help us figure out and understand what we are feeling. For instance, if there's an issue that might be weighing on your mind in your waking hours, your subconscious may generate a dream about it—either through overt imagery or more subtle references (e.g., dreaming of walking through a dark, cold, vast space might correlate with a move to a new and unfamiliar city).

But while emotional processing might be occurring at a largely subconscious level, the fact that we remember so few of our dreams is a convincing argument against this theory. Additionally, there is no evidence that those who recall their dreams with more facility are better off in some way than those who do not.

Random activation theory suggests that dreams have no meaning or purpose, that they are the result of random neurons in the brain firing and are just the by-product of what happens to the brain when it goes to sleep. At the same time, it's intriguing to consider why we have evolved to have REM sleep, which uses up a lot of energy—almost as much as being awake. In and of itself, this suggests that there must be a good reason why we dream.

Another set of theories says that dreams evolved because they helped early humans perform more efficiently during the day, perhaps by letting people rehearse situations and how they would deal with them in a kind of virtual reality simulator. The threat-simulation theory suggests that dreams are a safe way to practice how to deal with threatening situations.

Whether dreams have an evolutionary function is still a matter of speculation. The most common theory has been that dreaming is a way to sift through all the information we encounter on a daily basis. The human brain is met with hundreds of thousands of stimuli per day, ranging from sensory details to complex problems. As we dream, the brain is given a way to process this information, deciding what is important and what is not. Studies, in fact, have indicated that during intense periods of learning in our waking lives, dream activity increases while we sleep. Thus, dreams are believed to convert short-term memories into long-term ones, and to clear out the software that has been accumulated over the course of a busy day.

At the same time, many of the dreams we have—even if they were to be approached metaphorically—have little to do with

Idle time

Another collection of theories is that dreaming resembles what a computer does when you are not using it. If a computer sits idle long enough, it switches into a kind of housekeeping mode, where it cleans its memory, updates programs, and does other offline processing. According to this school of thought, dreams help your mind clean up difficult emotions and thoughts, providing psychological healing, and they also help with learning by filing away new memories and knowledge in the right places.

actual events we experienced during our day. While the story presented may be plausible, it still remains, by and large, in the realm of the imagination.

While dream researchers have yet to come up with a unifying argument about their function, dreams nevertheless remain an intriguing (and often inspiring) aspect of our lives. As long as we have a relatively small amount of information on how and why the brain functions as it does, dreams will persist as one of the more enigmatic workings of the psyche.

Why do we forget?

We forget so that we can remember other things better and more efficiently.

Forgetfulness is irritating, damaging, and distressing—but it may also be necessary for basic survival.

Explanations for forgetting depend partly on explanations for memory. The most popular model of memory has three stages, and forgetting can take place at all three. In the first stage, information floods into your brain via your senses, and the most important information is held briefly in a very short-term zone called the sensory register. If you don't pay any attention to this information, it will almost immediately disappear through a process called decay. Decay is what happens when nerve cells stop firing in a certain pattern, and that pattern is lost.

The second stage of memory formation is called short-term memory. If you are trying to remember a phone number, short-term memory is where you hold it. Again, if you don't make an effort or the information is not memorable, it will decay or simply be replaced by the next bit of input that comes into your brain. In both this case and the previous one, you forget something because you never stored it as a memory to begin with.

The final stage of memory formation is long-term memory, in which a memory is laid down in your brain as a more or less permanent trace. It seems likely that once a memory is laid down like this, it lasts forever unless some physical damage actually destroys the nerve cells involved in the memory. But just because a memory is stored somewhere in your brain, it doesn't mean you can remember it. If you can't get hold of it, it means you've forgotten it, and there are lots of reasons for this.

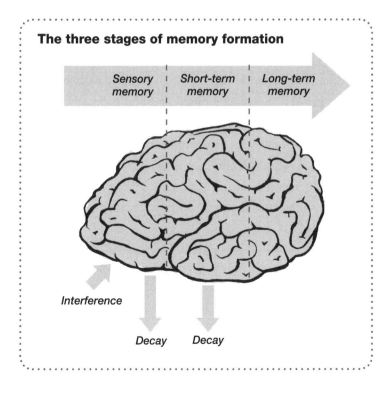

The three stages of memory formation

Sensory memory *Short-term memory* *Long-term memory*

Interference

Decay *Decay*

One reason is known as interference. This occurs when other memories interfere with the one you are trying to remember. For instance, if you are trying to remember what you had for dinner two days ago, the memory of what you ate yesterday might interfere.

Decay and interference explain how forgetting might help us to survive. Decay means that our brains don't store every single thing that happens, only the ones that stand out as the most important. This helps us to focus on significant survival factors, such as where we live and where to find food.

Interference makes it hard to remember everything, but by forgetting certain things, we stop them from accumulating and blocking out the most salient events and details. In other words, a good memory is a selective memory, which requires forgetting. It's much more important to remember what you ate at the meal that made you sick three years ago than it is to remember exactly what you had to eat three nights ago (unless it was the exact same thing—in which case, watch out!).

Perhaps what is really amazing isn't how much we forget, but how much we can remember. No one knows for sure how much information the human brain can hold, but most estimates agree that your memory can hold around 2.5 million gigabytes of information. A digital video recorder with the same capacity could hold 3 million hours of television programs. You would have to leave the television running continuously for more than 300 years to use up all that storage.

Why can't we fly?

We can't fly because we are too heavy and too weak. (Sometimes the truth hurts.)

Birds, bats, and insects fly, so why can't we? The simplest answer is that we are basically too large.

Why does size matter? In order to fly, you need to overcome the force of gravity. Flying animals generate lift (upward force) by moving their wings through the air, but to move their wings, they need another force known as thrust. You need muscles to provide thrust. The bigger and heavier you are, the more thrust you need to produce and the bigger your muscles have to be.

Although bigger muscles tend to produce more power, the relationship between muscle size and power is not straightforward. A muscle that is twice as big does not produce twice as much power. This is because muscle strength depends on the cross-section of the muscle rather than its overall size, so that while the mass of the muscle increases to the power of three, strength only increases to the power of two. In other words, to have a muscle that is four times stronger, you need one that is eight times bigger.

This is why flight is possible for relatively small animals, but gets increasingly difficult as body size increases. Large birds like the albatross and the condor are not strong enough to do much wing flapping and mostly rely on gliding flight.

According to Rhett Allain, associate professor of physics at Southeastern Louisiana University, a bird as big as an average-sized man would need wings about 23 feet across, but such wings would weigh a lot. To flap a pair of wings that size hard enough to lift around 220 pounds of weight (what the average man would roughly weigh if he had such wings) would require muscles many times stronger than the human arm and chest muscles. Also, because strength does not increase as quickly as mass, the muscles in question would be unfeasibly huge, adding yet more weight to the imaginary birdman.

This wide range of adaptations probably explains how some prehistoric birds, and possibly some prehistoric reptiles, managed to be as big or even bigger than humans. Quetzalcoatlus, a pterosaur from the Cretaceous era (about 67 million years ago), had a wingspan of more than 9 feet and may have weighed up to 220 pounds. It was the largest flying animal of all time, but possibly not the heaviest. That accolade belongs to the giant teratorn, *Argentavis magnificens*, a vulture-like bird from the Miocene era 6 to 8 million years ago, with a wingspan of about 24.5 feet and a weight of around 265 pounds.

> ### *Taking wing*
>
> *Birds also have a host of other adaptations to help them fly. They keep body weight down with hollow bones. They maintain a very high metabolism with better lungs than mammals, and they use feathers to keep in body heat. They have very large chest muscles and very large keel bones for the muscles to fix onto.*

These monsters could probably barely fly and must have relied almost exclusively on gliding. The fact that they match up with our imaginary birdman with respect to weight and wingspan suggests that if we could manage to get airborne, gliding would be relatively easy. In fact, humans with wing suits can already manage glides of over 10 miles.

Why are men bigger than women?

As strange as it may sound, it is likely the case that men are typically bigger than women today because our ape ancestors were polygynous.

Polygyny translates to "having many wives." In terms of human evolution, it means that a prehistoric apeman had lots of mates, and he had to fight other apemen to keep them. This supposedly explains why men are 8 percent taller and 15 to 20 percent bigger than women. However, there are lots of other theories, and some of them lead to interesting conclusions.

Differences in body size are an example of sexual dimorphism. In the world of large mammals—and particularly in the world of our closest relatives, the great apes (chimpanzees, gorillas, and orangutans)—sexual dimorphism in body size seems to be related to how animals choose and keep their mates.

Chimpanzees tend to live in mixed groups of males and females, where different male chimpanzees can mate with different female chimpanzees. Gorillas, on the other hand, have a setup whereby one alpha gorilla, a silverback, has a harem of female gorillas that he jealously presides over. If another male comes along and tries to poach one of his mates, the silverback tries to fight him off.

This variation in sexual behaviour explains why there isn't a big difference between male and female chimpanzees in terms of size, while there is a marked difference between male and female gorillas. Male gorillas have to be bigger so they can effectively guard their harems from potential intruders, whereas among chimpanzees, size is less important than other factors (such as intelligence, perhaps).

Humans and apes shared a common ancestor millions of years ago, so we probably evolved sexual dimorphism according to the same principles. The fossil record shows that today's body-size differences between men and women evolved at least 150,000 years ago and probably earlier.

What do differences in size between men and women say about the sexual behavior of early humans? Body-size differences in humans are smaller than in any of the other great apes, so the traditional explanation is that early humans were the most monogamous of the bunch; in other words, they were lovers rather than fighters. But they couldn't have been completely monogamous, or differences in size would never have evolved between men and women.

Not everyone agrees with the details of this explanation, however. Some have focused on the fact that although men and women are not that different in size (especially compared to other great apes), there is a huge difference between them in terms of muscles and strength. Men have 60 percent more muscle than women. Their arm muscles are 80 percent bigger, which is similar to the difference between male and female gorillas. On average, men's upper body strength is 90 percent greater than women's, and the average man is stronger than 99.9 percent of women.

What does all this mean? According to one explanation, it proves that men evolved to be fighters rather than lovers. Men are so much stronger than women because they had to evolve to be able to fight for their mates. The strongest men won the fights as well as the women, so genes for male strength were passed on to the next generation.

One-woman man?

We know from looking at societies throughout history and around the world that five out of six of all known societies are polygamous; divorce and remarriage, under some circumstances, are allowed in all human cultures. There is no reason to think things were any different for early humans, so early man probably had to be a bit of a bully when it came to grabbing and keeping a mate.

If you think that's a convincing argument, consider that there is a slight problem with this explanation. Genetic studies show that genes for size and strength are passed on equally to both sons and daughters. Body size differences between men and women cannot be passed on to the next generation consistently, since bigger men will yield bigger male and female offspring.

The difference in male and female body sizes

Men are roughly 8 percent taller than women and 15 to 20 percent bigger.

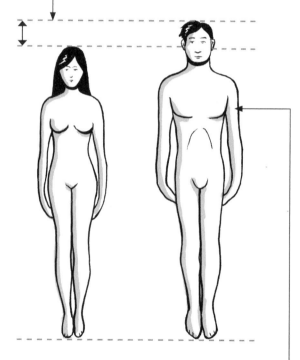

Men have 60 percent more muscle than women. Male arm muscles are 80 percent bigger.

If this is true, what is the explanation for men being bigger than women? According to a radical theory put forward by Satoshi Kanazawa and Deanna Novak, it's not that men are bigger than women, but that women are smaller than men—and more specifically, that women could conceivably grow to be as big as men, but for some reason, they stop growing earlier and end up with smaller bodies.

Their argument is that in a polygamous society, a woman had the best chance of securing a good mate by hitting puberty as early as possible. When a girl hits puberty, she essentially stops growing, and this is what restricts the height and size of women. (On average, women hit puberty a year or two earlier than men.) What determines how soon a girl hits puberty? Apparently, one of the major factors is how much time she spends with her father growing up. Girls with fathers who are heavily involved in their upbringing tend to delay puberty longer than girls with absent fathers. And particularly in early societies, where a woman may have depended on a strong male protector to keep her safe from intruders and predators, the absence of a father figure would be compensated for by her child-bearing ability—which would make her a desirable mate.

Why can't we photosynthesize?

We can't photosynthesize because we don't have chloroplasts, and we wouldn't get enough food out of photosynthesis to make it worthwhile, anyway.

The simple answer to why we can't photosynthesize is that we don't have any of the biological equipment necessary for the process. However, things become more complex when we consider that there are certain animals, including at least one vertebrate, that *can* photosynthesize.

In plants, photosynthesis takes place in special units inside the cell called plastids. Plastids containing chlorophyll, the green pigment that captures light for photosynthesis, are called chloroplasts. Humans can't make plastids, as we don't have the genes for this process.

It turns out that plants originally didn't have the genes for it either, so 1.5 billion years ago, they found some bacteria that did have the genes, and invited them over—forever. Plastids were originally photosynthetic bacteria called cyanobacteria, which took up residence inside other cells in a symbiotic (mutually beneficial) relationship. The cyanobacteria benefited from having a safe home with strong cell walls and a constant supply of water; their new hosts benefited from the sugars produced by the cyanobacteria. It was the beginning of a beautiful friendship, and now, 1.5 billion years later, the algae and plants that resulted from this union have conquered the world.

Living on borrowed plastids

If plants are playing host to someone else's chlorophyll, why can't we? There are many species of sea slug that eat algae, suck out their plastids, and give them new homes in their skin. They are able to keep the plastids alive for up to 10 months before they must consume more algae to replace them. Sea slugs that do this can live for up to 9 months without eating, relying on photosynthesis to feed them instead.

Even more intriguing, biologists have recently discovered that the spotted salamander (*Ambystoma maculatum*) can also play host to photosynthesizing guests inside its own cells. This is an exciting discovery because vertebrates (animals with backbones, such as salamanders and humans) have immune systems that are supposed to stop foreign cells from living inside their bodies. If salamanders can overcome this barrier, is it possible that humans can? With a bit of genetic tinkering, we might be able to engineer humans with plastids in their skin cells, so that they can photosynthesize and enjoy a supply of free sugar whenever the sun shines.

All the same, even if we could do this, it probably wouldn't be worth it. Humans don't have that much skin to photosynthesize with, and photosynthesis is not a particularly efficient process. According to one analysis, a photosynthesizing human lying naked in the sun at midday for an hour would produce just 15 calories of energy, equivalent to about a sixth of an apple. Humans need around 2,400 calories per day, so in order to survive by photosynthesis alone, a "green" person would have to sunbathe for 150 hours a day!

Why do men go bald?

Men probably go bald because prehistoric women simply preferred older men.

There are 193 species of monkeys and apes in the world today, but only one of them is hairless: us. This unusual fact led anthropologist Desmond Morris to come up with his famous phrase, "the naked ape." In fact, humans are not completely naked; we have several patches of hair, most notably on top of our heads. The average person has around 100,000 hairs on his or her head; blondes have finer, more numerous hairs, while redheads have the thinnest hair.

On average you can expect to drop about 62 of these hairs every day, but you can also expect to grow about the same number of new ones. As you get older, this cycle of loss and regrowth changes: Hairs are lost more quickly, while new ones grow more slowly. For a sizeable minority of the population, almost all of them male, the cycle stops completely, and lost hairs are never replaced. The naked ape becomes the bald ape.

One in 6 men goes bald, while 1 in 20 has a receding hairline by the time of his 21st birthday. Why is this?

Certain medications—as well as hormonal changes, illnesses, and even shocks—can cause hair loss in humans, but most men and women lose their hair as a result of genetic causes inherited from both the male and the female sides of the family. But since genes for baldness are so prevalent, that begs the question, what possible evolutionary advantage does baldness provide?

A bald statement

Sociobiologists Frank Muscarella and Michael Cunningham have discovered that women associate bald men with greater social maturity, wisdom, and calmness, and this fits with the general social stereotype that links baldness and wisdom. Muscarella and Cunningham suggest that some of our apewomen ancestors found these "bald" qualities more attractive than the immature aggressiveness of younger, hairier apemen, and this explains why baldness not only survived but thrived.

Some other apes and monkeys also go bald, and in chimpanzees, there seems to be a relationship between social status and baldness. Bald chimpanzees tend to be respected as older males. Perhaps baldness in humans evolved along similar lines.

The stages of male pattern baldness

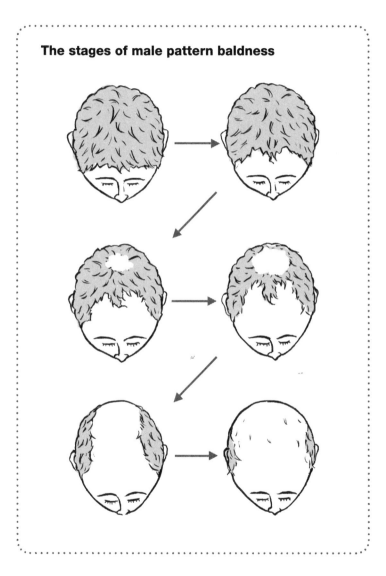

According to at least one controversial theory, baldness is not really genetic and has nothing to do with evolution. Scientist Armando José Yañez Soler suggests that baldness is the result of the wrong type of haircut, which stops hairs from rubbing against each other, which in turn damages the hair follicles and sets the unfortunate recipient of this pattern on the path to baldness.

Why do men have nipples?

Men have nipples because women do.

The importance of nipples in women is obvious: They deliver milk to suckling babies—up to about 1.5 pints a day! Other mammals manage even more impressive feats of lactation. In 2010 a cow from Wisconsin with the catchy name of Ever-Green-View My 1326-ET produced over 175 pints of milk a day for a year! (Cows normally manage around 55 pints a day.)

However, nipples appear to serve no purpose at all in men. Having nipples is part of what defines a mammal, but not all male mammals have nipples. Stallions (male horses) don't have nipples, and neither do male rats or mice.

Men probably have nipples because there isn't a good enough reason for them not to. When embryos are developing in the womb, they start off fairly unisex—both male and female embryos begin developing the same body structures, and these include nipples, which appear around the fourth week of development. By the seventh week, the baby's body begins to assume one sex or another as the sex hormones kick in; among males, the vaginal labia fuse to form the scrotum and the clitoris develops into the penis.

Nipples are not sex-linked body features in the same way as the genitals, so no signals arrive to cause the developing male embryo to lose them. If having nipples were a significant cause of problems for men, or in any way affected their survival and chances of generating offspring, there would have been pressure via natural selection for them to be lost. But this obviously hasn't been the case, so there has been no reason for men to evolve some special mechanism to lose their nipples during the development of the embryo.

So, ultimately, men have nipples because all embryos have them, and all embryos have them because the female ones will need them later.

But this doesn't offer a complete explanation. Male nipples are fully formed and are capable of becoming functional. During pregnancy and birth, a baby is exposed to heavy doses of its mother's hormones, and sometimes high levels of female sex hormones activate the breasts of boy babies so that they lactate when they are born. There is also a medical condition called gynecomastia, which leads to the enlargement of male breasts and can cause milk to leak from the nipples. Men can also develop breast cancer.

So why spend energy and resources on nipples that can work but rarely do and that can also be the cause of illness? Well, that's the enduring question . . .

Why are babies and puppies considered universally cute?

Babies and puppies are considered cute because we are hardwired to respond positively to faces with big eyes but otherwise small features.

Women between the ages of 19 and 26 might be the group that responds most strongly to babies; if a young woman sees a baby, her pupils dilate, and it takes just a seventh of a second for the parts of her brain involved with the feelings you get when you see something you really like to light up.

All the same, almost everyone is a sucker for puppies, kittens, seal cubs, and other baby animals. Even tiny crocodiles or baby skunks seem cute. But what do we mean by cute, and why is it so appealing?

Cuteness is very strongly linked to neoteny, a biological term for when creatures keep features associated with very early stages of development. These features are strong signals that the creature in question is young and defenseless and needs looking after.

The most obvious neotenous features are those that are apparent in the face. Young creatures of most species tend to have disproportionately big heads compared to their bodies, and to have big eyes compared to their heads. In humans, babies have eyes that are almost adult sized, but their heads are smaller and their bodies relatively tiny. The eyes don't grow much, but the rest of the body does, so by the time someone reaches adulthood, their eyes are proportionally much smaller.

The cut-off point for baby cuteness is around four and a half years old; children older than this are no longer seen as cute in the same way and do not trigger the same automatic responses from the adults looking at them. This age marks the point at which their features cease to appear neotenous.

For a lucky few, neoteny and its benefits extend into adulthood. Adults with features such as big eyes and small noses are generally viewed as more good looking, and men particularly find women with these features more attractive. The effects of neoteny can also cross species barriers so that humans respond to neoteny in other animals—hence, the perceived cuteness of puppies and kittens.

Why should we find cuteness so appealing and attractive? It seems to be hardwired into our brains as a means for making sure that we bond with and look after very young, helpless babies.

What does this have to do with men finding neotenous women sexy? Men probably evolved to be sexually drawn to those features that signal that a woman is young and fertile—and nothing signals youth like neoteny. Of course, neoteny signals

Disney babies

Other infantile features include button noses, small ears and chins, and rounded foreheads and faces. Most babies have these features, so we see them as being cute. This is why Barbie and Mickey Mouse both have enormous eyes. Such cuteness has real benefits. Cute babies get more attention and are more likely to be looked after. Babies with tiny eyes, flat foreheads, and square faces unfortunately tend to get less attention.

too much youth and it doesn't make evolutionary sense for men to find prepubescent girls attractive—but this may be an example of runaway sexual selection. This describes occurrences where one sex starts evolving certain features that indicate superior qualities, but once they get going, there is a sort of arms race that drives such features to exaggerated lengths. This is why, for instance, male moose have such huge antlers, and possibly why men have evolved such a hyperbolic desire for neotenous sexual features.

PHYSICS
AND
SPACE

Why does E=mc²?

$E=mc^2$ because mass and energy are two sides of the same coin.

Albert Einstein's famous equation is a mathematical way to express something known as the equivalence of mass and energy. Although in everyday life, we think of mass and energy as being two fundamentally different principles, physicists actually consider them to be different properties of the same principle.

In Einstein's equation, the E stands for energy, m stands for mass, and c stands for the speed of light. His equation says that mass and energy are interchangeable, and if you want to figure out how much energy is equivalent to a given amount of mass (or vice versa), you do the conversion by multiplying or dividing by the speed of light (c) squared. Often, the speed of light is measured in miles per second, so that $c^2 = 186,282$ x $186,282 =$ more than 21.5 million miles per second, which is a lot. But you can set the units in the equation to be what you want. (For more on this, see "Why can't we travel faster than the speed of light?" on page 170.) If you set them so that $c=1$, then $E=mc^2$ becomes $E=m1^2$. The square of 1 is 1, so this is just the same as saying $E=m$, or energy = mass.

Einstein worked out his equation after he realized that an object becomes heavier when it gains energy (technically, it becomes more massive, because weight and mass are not the same thing, but for everyday colloquial purposes we can say "heavier"). This means that when you sunbathe and heat up, you get heavier. When a cube of water freezes into ice, it gets lighter. But the amounts involved are so minute that you can't detect them.

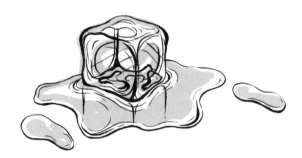

When you sunbathe and heat up, you get heavier. When a cube of water freezes into ice, it gets lighter.

To work out how much mass you get from a given amount of energy, you simply rearrange Einstein's equation. Instead of $E=mc^2$, write it as $M=E/c^2$. In other words, you have to divide energy by the square of c, the speed of light, which is a huge quantity, so you end up with an almost negligible amount of mass as the result.

For instance, a charged-up battery weighs about 0.0000000001 grams more than a battery that has been discharged. If you heat up a gold bar weighing a kilogram by 50°F, it gains about 0.000000000014 g. There are other types of energy apart from heat and chemical energy. To make something move, you give it kinetic energy. Every time you throw a ball, the ball gains kinetic energy and gets a tiny bit heavier. When a pitcher throws a baseball at 100 miles per hour, the ball gets 0.000000000002 g heavier. The fact that things get heavier as they get faster is very important to the question of why nothing can travel faster than light.

This relationship also works the other way around: Mass is equivalent to energy, so when something gets less massive, it releases energy. We can say that the mass has been converted to energy. And because you can work out how much energy is gained by multiplying the mass by the speed of light squared, you can see that even a tiny amount of mass has the capacity to be converted into a lot of energy. This inverse relationship between mass and energy is the basis of the nuclear bomb, and also of the nuclear-fusion reaction that powers the sun. The energetic content of just 2 pounds of matter would be enough to lift the population of the earth into space. If you were converted entirely into energy, you would explode more powerfully than thirty nuclear bombs.

Why do some objects float?

An object floats if it weighs less than the liquid that occupies the same amount of space.

Ever wonder why some objects float and others sink? When an object is less dense than water, it is buoyant. The "object" in question refers to an object in its entirety—this is why a ship can float even though it is made of iron, which is denser than water. The overall density of the ship is reduced because the iron also encloses a lot of air, which has a considerably lower density than water. The *Titanic* weighed 46,000 tons, but it floated because the water it displaced weighed even more. If the *Titanic* had been loaded up with lead, it would have sunk. Indeed, when an iceberg made a hole in the side and the *Titanic* filled up with water, it lost its buoyancy and sank.

The least buoyant material in the universe is the material that makes up a neutron star. It is the densest material known, and indeed, the densest material that can exist before turning into a black hole. A piece of neutron star the size of a sugar cube weighs more than the entire human race. According to the National Aeronautics and Space Administration (NASA), a neutron star weighs 1.4 to 5 times more than the sun. If our sun was as dense as a neutron star, it would be crammed into a space smaller than Mount Everest!

Take the weight off

If you've ever lamented the fact that you can't fly or walk on water, know that there are places in the world where you can still get a fair dose of buoyancy. Case in point: the Dead Sea, a salt lake on the border between Jordan, Israel, and the West Bank. Because six times more salt is dissolved in it than in ordinary seawater, the water in the Dead Sea is denser, which makes you more buoyant. In fact, the content of the Dead Sea is 29 percent salt, as opposed to the 4 percent that makes up the earth's oceans. This is why, despite your aquatic prowess, you will always float to the surface of the water like a cork.

Legend has it that the principle of buoyancy was first recognized by the ancient Greek mathematician Archimedes, prompting his famous "Eureka!" incident. The story goes that the king of Syracuse gave a lump of pure gold to a goldsmith to make a laurel wreath, but suspected the man of cheating him by stealing some of the gold and replacing it with silver. The king asked Archimedes to help unmask the fraud. Archimedes knew that a gold-silver alloy was less dense than pure gold, so if the wreath were actually impure, it would have to be more voluminous than a lump of gold that weighed the same. Unfortunately, there was no way to calculate the volume of a shape as complex as a wreath. Archimedes pondered the conundrum while relaxing in the bath, and noticed that the more he reclined, the more water spilled out of the bath. He realized that the volume of water that spilled from the bath was an exact measure of the volume of space he took up, and that here was a principle that could be used to determine the volume of the wreath. He was so excited that he leaped naked from the bath and exclaimed, "Eureka!" (Greek for "I've got it!") and capered down the street.

In the legend, Archimedes put a lump of pure gold weighing the same as the wreath into a bowl filled to the brim with water. He then removed the gold and immersed the wreath. The bowl overflowed, proving that the wreath had a greater volume, and therefore, lower density than the pure gold—so it must be an alloy. The guilty goldsmith got his comeuppance.

While it's a nice anecdote, it's probably not based on fact. Commentators since Galileo have pointed out that the difference in volume between the wreath and the lump of gold would be so small that this method would not actually work in practice. However, it is known from Archimedes' extant writings that he definitely explored the principle of buoyancy, and so could in theory have arrived at a cunning water displacement–based solution to the puzzle of the wonky wreath.

Why do apples fall down?

Apples fall because they are pulled by gravity toward the center of the earth.

Isaac Newton famously conceived of the force of gravity when struck on the head by a falling apple—or so the legend goes. Newton wasn't the first person to think about gravity, however; anyone can see that things fall down when you drop them. Newton's breakthrough was to realize that this was a fundamental and unilateral force of nature, affecting everything from the fall of an apple to the orbit of the moon around the earth. In the summer of 1666, Newton was sitting in his garden when he saw an apple fall from a tree and hit the ground. At this time, he was thinking deeply about what kept the moon in its orbit, and it suddenly occurred to him that there must be a relationship between the force that pulled the apple to Earth and the same force that pulled the moon toward the earth. He was even able to work out just how strong that force must be, and how it got weaker as the distance increased between an object and the larger body that exerted the force.

The ultimate answer that Newton came up with is that gravity is a force of attraction between any and all objects, and that its strength is determined by the size of the objects and the distance between them. There is a force of gravity between an apple and another apple, but because they are so small, it is barely detectable. The earth, in comparison, is large, so for objects directly in its field, the force of gravity between them is quite strong—strong enough to make an apple that comes loose from its tree accelerate toward the ground at a rate of about 32 feet per second per second (i.e., every second the apple falls, its speed increases by about 32 f/s). Bigger planets have stronger gravity; on Jupiter, an apple would accelerate toward the ground at about 83 f/s^2, and on the surface of the sun an apple would fall at about 900 f/s^2.

But as universal as the theory of gravity may be, there's still been room for improvement and expansion. About 240 years after Newton, Albert Einstein came along and slightly modified our picture of gravity. He posited that the universe consists of a space-time continuum, and that objects cause bulges in the fabric of space-time, much like balls sitting on a rubber sheet. A big ball, like the earth, causes a very deep bulge, so that a smaller ball, like an apple, will roll down the slope into the bulge. The steepness of the bulge is what determines how quickly other balls will fall into it—in other words, how strong the gravitational force is. So Einstein might have said that the reason an apple falls to the ground is that it is simply following the contours of space-time, which are deformed by the mass of the earth.

Why are there so many planets in our solar system?

There are multiple planets in our solar system because our sun, after coming into existence, grew slowly enough to allow ample space and time for a large number of planets to form.

There are eight planets in our solar system. The planets probably formed from something called an accretion disc. This launched life billions of years ago in a primal, formless soup of gas and dust floating in space. Something disturbed the cloud—possibly shockwaves from a nearby exploding star—and pushed some of the gas and dust closer together. When areas of the cloud concentrated in one spot, this new gravitational pull became stronger than the rest of the cloud, and the concentrated area was quickly pulled into a big, gaseous ball.

As the particles of the ball got squished together, the ball began to heat up, becoming a protostar, or a young sun. What was left of the cloud got squeezed into a disc that rotated around the protostar, and this disc cooled down enough for the gas within it to solidify into ice and rock particles. The accretion disc gets its name from the way some of the larger particles in it started to accrete (i.e., pick up) other, smaller particles. They grew into large, asteroid-like objects, called planetesimals, and these in turn collided with each other; in our solar system, this process resulted in the eight planets we know today.

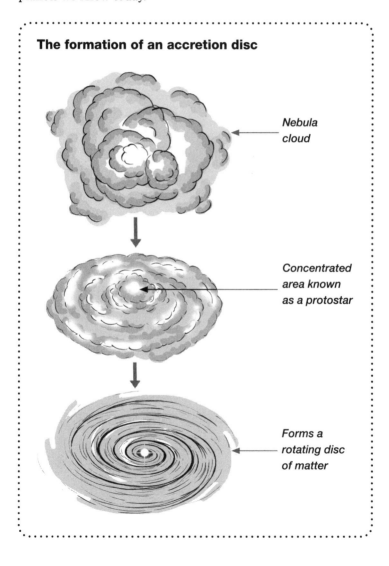

The formation of an accretion disc

Nebula cloud

Concentrated area known as a protostar

Forms a rotating disc of matter

If the protostar had been bigger, it might have split into a double star, and the two stars would probably have destroyed a significant portion of the accretion disc, leaving less material for planets. And if the protostar had been hotter, the accretion disc would never have cooled down enough for gas to solidify into ice and rock, meaning the planets might not have formed.

The Pluto formerly known as planet

There used to be nine planets in our solar system, but in 2006 the International Astronomical Union (IAU) decided that Pluto is too small to be considered a planet and should be reclassified as a dwarf planet or a Kuiper belt object. The Kuiper belt is a zone of large objects in the outer reaches of the solar system, some of which are the same size as, or bigger than, Pluto. The IAU concluded that if Pluto were to be classified as a planet, so should these other objects, and our solar system could be said to have a dozen or more planets.

There are probably a number of other factors that, if they had turned out differently, may have changed the number of our solar system's planets. For instance, if Jupiter's orbit had been just a little different, it would have knocked most of the other planets out of orbit and sent them hurtling into space.

Why is the universe expanding?

The universe is expanding because it is filled with more dark (invisible) energy than visible matter.

The ultimate cause for the expansion of the universe is inflationary pressure from the Big Bang, thanks to which the universe is now almost 100 billion light-years across, even though it is only 13.7 billion years old. (Note that a single light-year is 5.9 trillion miles!)

According to the Big Bang theory, the universe started off as an infinitely small point and expanded incredibly quickly in a process called inflation. To go from essentially nothing to about the size of a large rubber ball took just 10^{34} seconds (that's 0.000000000000 0000000000000000000000001 seconds!). To give you an idea of the kind of speed we're talking about, this early universe expanded at three trillion trillion trillion times the speed of light.

As a result of the Big Bang, lots of matter appeared in the form of gas, dust, stars, galaxies, black holes, and the list goes on. Matter causes gravity, and gravity is a force that attracts objects in space to each other. So if the universe were made only of matter, then gravity would be acting against the outward pressure of Big Bang inflation, working to bring objects closer together.

In the dark

To account for the continuing expansion of the universe, scientists have relied upon the hypothesis of "dark energy." According to this hypothesis, 70 percent of the universe must be made of dark energy, and another 25 percent a form of invisible matter known as dark matter. According to NASA, dark energy is the outward force that opposes gravity and contributes to the expansion of the universe. Data about the rotation of galaxies reveals that the outer parts of a galaxy rotate faster than the inner parts. This would only make sense if there were a spherical distribution of matter in the galaxy, which isn't what we actually see. This means that there must be dark matter, which could be composed of exotic particles we are as of yet unaware of, or a number of stars that are too small to have ignited.

This means that all the visible matter in the universe, including the galaxies, stars, planets, black holes, and nebulae, adds up to just 5 percent of the universe. The dark energy is somehow causing the universe not just to expand, but to expand increasingly fast.

Clearly, this isn't happening. If we believed that the universe were primarily composed of matter, astronomers might expect to see the expansion of the universe slowing down, or even going into reverse—but in fact, they see the expansion accelerating.

This strongly suggests that the universe must be packed with another kind of energy that acts against gravity. Fair enough, but the major problem is nobody can see this energy, and nobody knows what it is.

How do astronomers know how much stuff actually makes up the universe? They measure something called cosmic microwave background radiation (CMBR), which is a remnant of the Big Bang, like a very faint echo from the beginning of time. The CMBR accounts for 99 percent of the radiation in the universe. You can see it for yourself by switching on an analog television set between channels; a very small fraction of the static you can see is caused by CMBR.

Why does the sea appear blue?

The sea appears blue because water absorbs more red and yellow light than blue light.

A glass of water looks colorless, but in fact it is a very light blue. If you have enough water in one place, as in the deep sea, this blue color becomes visible.

Sunlight falling on the sea is made up of white light, which comprises all the colors of the spectrum. Some of the sunlight reflects off the surface of the water; the rest of it passes into the water. The water molecules absorb certain colors or wavelengths of light more than others. The colors they absorb most are red, yellow, and green, and this leaves blue light. Some of this blue light keeps going down into the water, and some is scattered by the water molecules so that it rises from the water and meets your eyes. About 65 percent of the visible light entering the ocean is absorbed within the first 3 feet or so of water; less than 1 percent penetrates as far as about 100 yards, and this is entirely blue light.

But the sea is not always blue. Close to the coast it often looks green, and it is also possible to get red, yellow, and brown seas.

Muddying the waters

Close to the coast, there tends to be a lot more sediment (small particles of dirt) in the water because of all the dirt that washes off the land into the sea. This sediment changes the way light is absorbed and reflected; the floating specks of dirt tend to absorb red and blue light the most, leaving green light to reflect back out of the water and make coastal waters appear green.

These colors depend on the composition of the water and which colors of light the water absorbs or reflects.

Various other colors can be seen as the result of tiny plants floating in the water. Known as phytoplankton, these tiny plants use pigments such as chlorophyll to harvest sunlight, and they can stain the water. Green phytoplankton make the water look green, but phytoplankton come in many different colors, depending on the pigment used by each species. Some phytoplankton species use red pigments, and these are responsible for what are called red tides.

The seabed also affects water color if the sea is shallow enough for light to reach and reflect off it. In tropical areas with clear, shallow water, the ocean appears very light blue because of the color of the white sandy bottom mixing with the blue water.

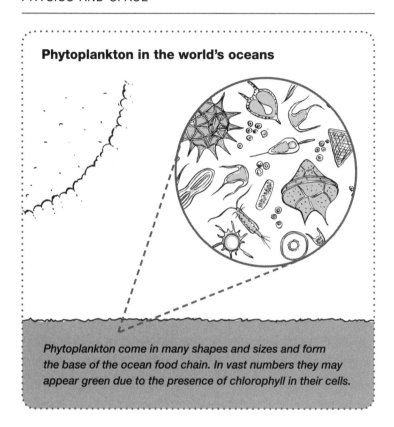

Phytoplankton in the world's oceans

Phytoplankton come in many shapes and sizes and form the base of the ocean food chain. In vast numbers they may appear green due to the presence of chlorophyll in their cells.

Water covers 71 percent of the earth's surface, and this is why the earth appears blue from space.

Why does the wind blow?

The wind blows because some parts of the earth's surface heat up more than other parts, causing air to rise, which draws in air from elsewhere.

Wind is the movement of air over the earth's surface. Air moves from one place to another to even out differences in pressure. If you are in New York or another location at sea level, there are about 7.5 miles of air piled up on top of you, and this mass of air presses down with an average pressure of 1 bar (1,000 mb), or 1 atmosphere. Where part of the earth's surface is hotter, the air above the surface is heated, and hot air rises. Rising air creates low pressure. Gases, such as air, flow from areas of high pressure to areas of low pressure.

Why do some parts of the earth's surface heat up more than others? Latitude (position relative to the equator and the poles) is a big influence, because the equator gets much more concentrated sunlight than the polar regions. Land and sea are other major influences—land heats up and cools down much faster than water, so that during the day the land tends to be hotter than the sea, and vice versa at night. Other influences include ocean currents, forests, and mountains.

Rise and fall

Heating at the equator creates a permanent band of low pressure around the earth known as the doldrums. Here, air is rising to the top of the atmosphere and spreading out. Meanwhile, at what are known as the horse latitudes, air is falling back to the earth, creating bands of high pressure. This air flows back toward the equator as the trade winds.

Global wind patterns

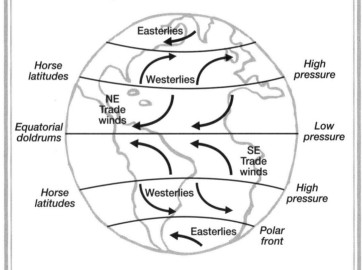

At the horse latitudes, westerlies blow toward the poles and the trade winds (winds blowing from the east) flow back toward the equator.

The rotation of the earth changes the direction of the wind and causes systems of high and low pressure to spin in enormous whirls known as cyclones and anticyclones. In tropical regions, these systems can turn into hurricanes, where the warm ocean pumps so much energy into the atmosphere that wind speeds reach up to about 75 miles per hour, or more. Hurricanes contain terrifying amounts of energy; in a single day, a hurricane releases enough energy to power the entire United States for 6 months, or provide a whole year of power for a country like Britain or France.

Over land, special types of storm clouds can create very concentrated whirls of wind called tornadoes. The highest wind speed ever measured was 318 mph during a tornado in Oklahoma in 1999, but the U.S. National Weather Service estimates that wind speeds can reach up to 500 mph in a tornado.

Why is the earth round?

The earth is round because gravity pulls with equal strength in all directions, so that any uneven bits are pulled back in line with all the other bits, creating a sphere.

Imagine a crowd of people concentrated in the middle of a field, each person tied to the others by a length of rope. Now imagine they all start running outward, pulling on the rope that binds them together. The crowd of people will quickly be pulled into a circle, and anyone who tries to move out of the circle will be pulled back in. This, in three dimensions, is what happens to the earth. It's called hydrostatic equilibrium.

In fact, this is the process that happens with all mass. However, you don't see the effects with all objects, because most of the ones around us exert a weak gravitational force. Your mobile phone, for instance, exerts gravity on itself and everything around it, but its gravitational pull is so incredibly tiny that you can't feel it, and it cannot possibly overcome the strength of the metal and plastic that give the phone its rectangular shape. But the larger an object gets, the stronger its gravity. Any asteroid bigger than about 600 miles across will collapse into a sphere under its own gravity. This is now one of the definitions of a planet, according to the International Astronomical Union.

In fact, the earth is not completely round. Once every 24 hours, it spins around an axis that runs through the poles, which means that the equator is moving much faster than the poles. With the surface of the earth at the equator moving at 1,040 miles per hour, there is a centrifugal force pressing outward, and this makes the earth bulge at the equator. The distance from the center of the earth to the equator is about 0.33 percent farther than the distance from the center of the earth to the poles, which means that the diameter of the earth from pole to pole is about 27 miles shorter than it is across the equator. So the top of Mount Everest is not the point on the earth's surface furthest from the center of the planet; that honor actually goes to Mount Chimborazo in Ecuador, which is almost directly on the equator. The relatively greater thickness at the center of the earth means that our planet is not a perfect sphere, but an oblate spheroid.

In addition, the earth has mountains, valleys, ocean trenches, and other wrinkles, so its surface is not smooth. But compared to the overall size of the earth, these areas are tiny. A billiard ball is smooth to within a tolerance of 0.22 percent, but the earth is smooth to within a tolerance of 0.17 percent, so if a galactic-sized giant came along and handled the earth, it would feel smoother than a billiard ball.

Why is there a dark side of the moon?

As a matter of fact, there isn't.

All parts of the moon, with the exception of the corners of some deep craters that are in permanent shadow, are illuminated by the sun half the time.

There is, however, a far side of the moon, which Earth-based observers never get to see, and which remained one of the great mysteries of nature until a Russian spacecraft orbited the moon in 1959.

Why do we only get to see one side of the moon? The moon is in a synchronous orbit around the earth; in other words, as the moon goes around the earth, it also rotates on its axis at exactly the right speed to ensure that the same side is always facing the earth.

This was not always the case. The moon was probably formed about 4.5 billion years ago, when a planet the size of Mars crashed into the earth and was blown into pieces. The rubble went into orbit around the earth and accreted together to form the moon, which, with a diameter of about 2,160 miles, is just over a quarter the size of the earth.

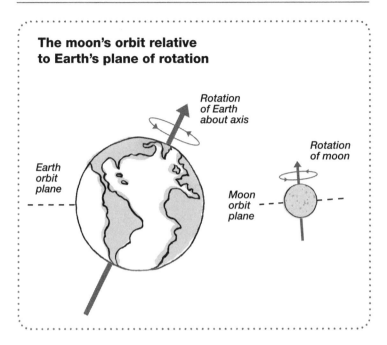

**The moon's orbit relative
to Earth's plane of rotation**

Rotation
of Earth
about axis

Rotation
of moon

Earth
orbit
plane

Moon
orbit
plane

At this time the moon was much closer to the earth and spun much faster, but the effects of the tides caused both the earth and its moon to slow down and move farther apart. Today they are about 238,855 miles apart, a distance that increases by 1.5 inches a year. If there were no moon, the earth would now be spinning about three times faster, giving us 1,095 days in a year, each day clocking just 8 hours long.

The same braking effect acted on the moon in the past, slowing its rotation until it reached what is called the tidal locking point, when its rotation became synchronous with its orbit, so that the same side always faces the earth.

Seeing in the dark

It could be said that the far side of the moon is at least meta-phorically valid, in that it has been invisible and mysterious—at least, up until recently. Spacecraft have photographed the far side of the moon extensively, starting with the Soviet probe Luna 3 *in 1959. But even though the far side of the moon remains largely unknown to us, the moon wobbles slightly as it spins, making a few degrees of the far side visible from the earth.*

So, what's on the far side of the moon? Mainly a lot of craters named after Soviet heroes because it was their scientists who got to assign names first, giving us features such as the Mendeleyev and the Korolev craters.

The far side is quite different from the near side, with fewer "seas" (large, dark, relatively smooth areas formed from floods of lava) and more rugged, cratered highlands. This is because the far side has a thicker crust than the near side. One recent discovery about the difference between the far and near sides of the moon is that the earth originally had two moons, which collided around 4.4 billion years ago. The smaller one was smeared across the face of what would become the far side, and the impact drove the young moon's magma across to the near side, where it produced a thinner crust and more frequent lava-flooding events.

Why does time only move forward?

Time moves forward because you can't unspill milk or unshatter a glass; in other words, time obeys the law of entropy.

One of the great conundrums of physics is explaining why time's arrow points forward. The arrow of time is an idea devised in 1927 by British physicist Arthur Eddington, who used it to describe the way time seems to move in only one direction. You can move from the past into the future, but not back the other way. If space and time together create four dimensions, time is the only dimension in which you can only travel in one direction.

All of the equations that physicists use to describe the universe, such as ones dealing with gravity and electromagnetism, work perfectly well in either direction. They are said to be symmetrical, and they don't seem to be affected by the direction of time's arrow. Yet time does have an arrow.

The answer to this mystery is the second law of thermodynamics, which states that entropy always increases. Entropy translates to disorder, or unusable energy. In a closed system, where you are not allowed to add any energy to what you started with, disorder will always increase. In real life, this means that if you spill milk from a jug, the milk cannot leap back into the jug, or if you drop a glass and it shatters, it will not reassemble itself and leap back into your hand. If you ran a film of either of these events, you would be able to tell whether it was running backward or forward, unlike the symmetrical equations mentioned above. This increase of entropy means that time can run in only one direction.

The irreversible nature of the second law of thermodynamics is probably linked to the origins of the universe itself, which started off incredibly small and dense, and has been expanding ever since. Immediately after the Big Bang, the universe had a low degree of entropy, and as time passed, its entropy increased and continues to increase. This is known as the cosmological arrow of time.

A possible fate for the universe is that it will eventually become completely disordered with maximum entropy, which means that all matter and energy will become evenly distributed. The available energy would end up spread thinly across the entire universe, so it would be very cold everywhere. This fate is sometimes called the heat death of the universe. An alternative fate is that the universe will stop expanding and go into reverse, a scenario called the Big Crunch. According to the premise of the Big Crunch, entropy might decrease and time might change direction!

Why do lightbulbs light up?

Lightbulbs light up because electrons have to squeeze through their narrow filament, forcing them to collide into the atoms of the filament, which makes them vibrate and give off heat and light.

An electrical circuit with a battery, wires, and a lightbulb is like an aquarium with a water pump, tubes, and a filter. The battery acts like a pump, forcing water around the tubes and through the filter, which is like a lightbulb. The tubes let the water flow quite easily, but the filter is narrow and partially blocked, so it is harder for the water to get through. Squeezing through causes the water to lose energy through friction.

In an electrical circuit, the electrons that carry the current are like the water. They can pass through the wires quite easily because they are made of copper and have a low resistance to electricity—but the filament is made of tungsten, a metal with a high resistance. Also, the filament is extremely long and thin; in a typical 60-watt bulb, the tungsten filament is more than 6 feet long but only a quarter of a millimeter thick, which makes it even more resistant. Resistance is a measure of how easily electricity can pass through something. The electrons work so hard to get through the tungsten that they pass energy to the atoms of the filament. As the tungsten atoms build up energy, they get excited, which makes them give off heat and light energy.

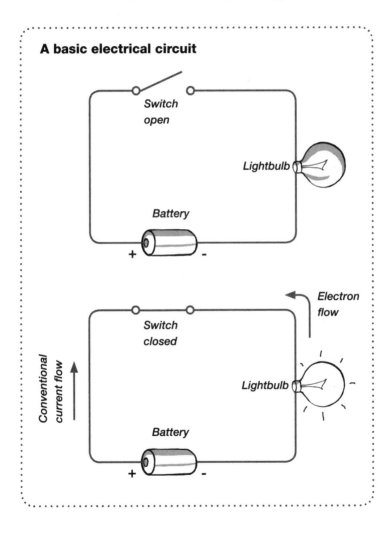

A basic electrical circuit

Switch
open

Lightbulb

Battery

+   −

Electron
flow

Switch
closed

Conventional
current flow

Lightbulb

Battery

+   −

Like most metals, tungsten has to be white hot before it gives off much light, so lightbulb filaments get to about 4,000°F. Even then, about 90 percent of their energy is given off as invisible infrared light (heat), so normal lightbulbs aren't very efficient at turning electricity into light.

They also tend to burn out quite quickly so they need replacing often; the United States alone spends about $1 billion buying 2 billion lightbulbs a year—that's 5.5 million lightbulbs a day! Lightbulbs can last a very long time, however. The longest-burning lightbulb is the Livermore Light in Fire Station 6, Livermore, California, which has been burning since 1901. So far, it has used up about as much energy as you would need to run a clothes dryer for 4 years.

Why split the atom?

The atom is worth splitting because it has the highest energy density of any fuel available.

Burning about 2 pounds of coal can power a 100-watt lightbulb for about 4 days, and about 2 pounds of uranium can power the lightbulb for just over 140 years. This means that, pound for pound, uranium provides 16,000 times more electricity than coal. Another way of saying this is that the energy density of uranium is 16,000 times higher than that of coal.

The reason that uranium has such a high energy density is because it is relatively easy to split an atom of uranium with a process known as nuclear fission. When an atom of uranium-235 splits into an atom of barium and an atom of krypton, a miniscule part of the original uranium atom is converted into energy. Einstein's famous $E=mc^2$ equation tells us that even a tiny bit of mass equals a colossal amount of energy.

Splitting the atom releases so much energy that from a single gram of uranium, it is possible to make one megawatt of energy per day. You would have to burn 600 gallons of oil to get the same amount of energy.

The enormous energy density of uranium has important consequences for the environment and energy security. Because fission produces no direct emissions (carbon dioxide, sulphur dioxide, nitrogen oxides, etc.), nuclear energy does not add to greenhouse gases. Fission does produce some radioactive waste, which poses its own special problems, but the amount of waste produced is relatively tiny. The waste per kilowatt-hour of electricity produced by a nuclear power plant is around 0.10 ounces. In contrast, for natural gas, the figure is about 400 pounds, and for coal it is a staggering 1.17 tons.

Also, because so little uranium fuel is needed to keep a nuclear plant running, it is easy for a country to get enough to supply most of its energy needs. Only 220 tons of milled uranium are needed to keep a 1,000-megawatt nuclear reactor going for a year, so a single warehouse can hold enough fuel to guarantee the energy security of an entire country for years. Since one of

Nuclear future

Some countries rely heavily on nuclear power. Worldwide, nuclear power through fission supplied about 13.5 percent of the world's electricity production in 2010, but in some countries the figure is much higher. France gets 77 percent of its energy from nuclear power.

the main causes of warfare, conflict, and terrorism in the world is control of energy supplies, specifically oil, switching to nuclear energy could make the world a much safer place.

The other reason to split the atom, though not considered tenable or smart by many, is to produce incredibly powerful and destructive weapons. The atomic bomb dropped on Hiroshima in 1945 was 2,000 times more powerful than the biggest bomb ever used up until then. The largest nuclear weapon ever created, the Soviet Tsar Bomba of 1961, was 10 times more powerful than all of the explosives used in World War II put together.

Why is the sky blue?

The sky is blue because air scatters blue light but lets other colors pass straight through.

Viewed from space, the sun is supposedly a peach-pinkish hue, while the sunlight that hits the earth is white. In scientific terms, color corresponds to a particular wavelength of light, so white light is assembled of a mixture of wavelengths. The colors that we see are the result of what happens to sunlight as it passes through the atmosphere, all 5,730 trillion tons of it—that's about 27.5 million tons of air for every square mile of the earth's surface.

If you were to look directly at the sun (which you should never do), you would see yellowish white light. This is what is left of the sunlight that is coming directly to your eyes after the wavelengths of blue have been scattered by hitting air molecules. The red and yellow light are hardly scattered and come directly down to the earth in a straight line. The blue light, on the other hand, bounces all over the sky, and some of it eventually reaches your eye. So if you look anywhere other than directly at the sun, you will see blue light.

As the sunlight, with its mixture of colors/wavelengths, passes through the atmosphere, it hits air molecules, and some of it gets

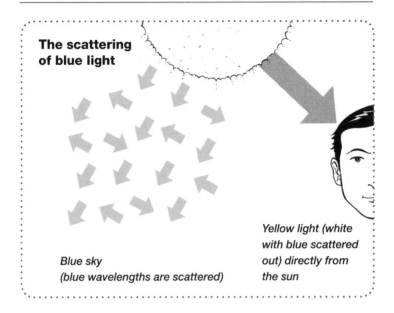

The scattering of blue light

Blue sky (blue wavelengths are scattered)

Yellow light (white with blue scattered out) directly from the sun

scattered. This effect is called Rayleigh scattering, after the British physicist John William Strutt, Lord Rayleigh (1842–1919), who devised the theory on why this happens. The amount of scattering that happens depends on the wavelength of the light and the size of the particles that are doing the scattering. Very tiny particles, like the oxygen and nitrogen molecules that make up 99 percent of the atmosphere, scatter short wavelengths of light (blue) but not long wavelengths (red). The same effect can be seen in smoke that is made up of very tiny particles, which is why tobacco smoke appears blue. This color is named after a different physicist, John Tyndall (1820–93), and is known as Tyndall blue. In fact, it was Tyndall who first explained why the sky is blue, even though Rayleigh gets all the glory.

Rayleigh scattering also indirectly explains why sunsets are red and orange. When the sun is going down over the horizon, the sunlight travels through much more air on its way to your eyes than when the sun is overhead. By the time the sunlight reaches your eyes, all the blue has been scattered, leaving only the orange and red end of the spectrum. This light gets scattered, but by larger dust particles rather than air molecules. Sunsets are a particularly vivid red and orange when the sky is full of dust, such as after a volcanic eruption.

On Mars the atmosphere is very thin, so there is relatively little Rayleigh scattering. But there is lots of dust in the air, so red light is scattered instead. This is why on Mars the sky appears red.

Why does ice float?

Ice floats because it is less dense than water, thanks to the hydrogen bonds between water molecules.

Water is one of the strangest chemicals in the universe, and many of its strangest features turn out to be essential to life as we know it. This is particularly evident in the unique property of water related to freezing. Unlike nearly every other liquid, water expands when it freezes into a solid by about 9 percent, making ice less dense than water.

This is odd, because what is supposed to happen when a liquid freezes is that all its atoms and molecules stop zooming around and settle down into a stable, regular pattern. Imagine trying to cram a lot of people into a phone booth. If they were jumping up and down and waving their arms around, you wouldn't be able to fit too many of them in, which would create a low density of people. This is normally what happens with the particles in a liquid, so they are less dense than solids. But if the people were standing still with their arms by their sides, you could pack a lot more of them in, and there would be a high density of people in the booth. So in effect, freezing a liquid makes it more dense.

Water is different because the H_2O molecules that make it up contain unusual properties. The single oxygen and two hydrogen atoms in each molecule share their electrons unevenly, and this turns the water molecule into a sort of a magnet, with one negatively charged end and two positively charged ends. Each of these ends can attract and stick to opposite charges, and this gives the water molecule the ability to form a type of bond called a hydrogen bond. In particular, each water molecule can form hydrogen bonds with up to four other water molecules.

In liquid water, the hydrogen bonding actually allows the molecules to get closer together than the particles that make up most other liquids, by about 15 percent. As water cools, its molecules have less energy and they slow down and cluster together, as with any other liquid. This continues until water reaches its maximum density at about 39°F, but below this, something unusual happens: Each water molecule starts to form all four of its possible hydrogen bonds, so that by the time water freezes at 32°F, the water molecules are locked into a rigid lattice with a much more open structure than the loose arrangements of molecules in liquid water.

Imagine that all the people in your crammed phone booth grab hold of one another by sticking their arms out straight. They are locked into a solid mass, but they end up further away from one another than if they were jiggling about with their arms by their sides. This is basically what happens with ice.

Ice saver

The lower density of ice makes life on Earth possible. If ice didn't float, it would sink. A pond would quickly freeze solid in winter as ice formed at the surface and then sank to the bottom, exposing more water at the top to freeze, and so on. Instead, the ice layer floats on top, insulating the rest of the pond. Any fish that live in the pond can survive because the bottom of the pond stays in liquid form.

On a much greater scale, this is what happens in winter in the oceans around the poles. The sea freezes into a layer of ice about 6 feet thick in the Arctic and about 10 feet thick in the Antarctic. The ice sheets grow until they cover about 12 percent of the surface of the oceans, extending over an area of some 6 million square miles of the Arctic Ocean, and 8 million square miles of the Antarctic.

The buoyancy of ice also has important consequences for shipping, as the *Titanic* learned. When glaciers feed into the sea, huge chunks of ice calve off the ends, forming icebergs that float in the ocean. (*Calving* refers to the sudden breaking away of a large sheet of ice from a glacier or iceberg.)

In the Arctic, about 12,000 icebergs calve off glaciers each year, weighing on average around 1.65 million tons, poking about 260 feet out of the water, and extending about 1,150 feet below the surface. Fortunately, relatively few of them reach the Atlantic, and they shrink by up to 90 percent by the time they do.

Why does iron stick to a magnet?

Iron sticks to a magnet because the magnetic field of the magnet turns the iron itself into another magnet.

A magnet has two ends, or poles, referred to as north and south. The north pole of one magnet is attracted to the south pole of another magnet. When an iron nail sticks to a magnet, it is because it has been magnetized, and the south pole of the nail is being attracted by the north pole of the magnet (or vice versa).

When a magnet turns a piece of iron into another magnet, this is called induced magnetism. Iron and other ferrous (ironlike) metals are said to be ferromagnetic because they have properties that enable them to be magnetically induced.

Induced magnetism occurs because a piece of iron is made up of thousands of regions, each of which is like a tiny magnet. Normally, these tiny magnetic regions, called domains, point in many different directions so that their combined magnetism cancels one another out, but when they are magnetically induced, the domains all turn around to point in the same direction.

A domain consists of a cluster of neighboring atoms that align to create a tiny magnet. About 6,000 domains fit onto the head of a pin. Each of these domains is made up of somewhere in the region of a quadrillion atoms (that's 1,000,000,000,000,000 atoms).

What makes the atoms in a domain magnetic? An atom is made up of a positively charged nucleus surrounded by negatively charged electrons. A magnetic field is produced by an electrical charge in motion, so as these electrons spin around, each of them creates its own tiny magnetic field. In most elements, different electrons produce magnetic fields in different directions and they cancel one another out, but in ferromagnetic elements—such as iron, cobalt, and nickel—the magnetic fields add up, and each atom becomes an atomic magnet. Millions of billions of these atomic magnets line up to become domains, and the domains can be induced to line up to turn an entire piece of ferrous metal into a magnet.

Take the magnet away from the iron nail and you take away the magnetic field that is inducing the domains in the nail to line up. The domains go back to pointing in random directions, and the nail stops being a magnet.

Some metal alloys, such as steel, keep their magnetism after being induced. This is why you can turn a steel sewing needle into a compass needle by stroking it with a magnet.

The reason compass needles point north is that the earth itself is a giant magnet (probably thanks to liquid iron in the earth's core), but not a very strong one.

Why can't we travel faster than light?

We can't travel faster than light because the faster things travel, the heavier they get.

Science fiction wouldn't get very far without warp speed, hyperspace, or any of the other ways that spaceships travel faster than light. Unfortunately, physics indicates that science fiction can never become science fact, because we can never travel faster than light.

Actually, it is possible to travel faster than light—in some situations you could outrun a beam of light on a motorbike. This is because light slows down a lot when it travels through other substances. Light slows down to less than half its normal speed when passing through diamond. The slowest speed ever recorded for light is 38 mph, which was while it was traveling through an exotic form of matter called a Bose-Einstein condensate of rubidium.

What physicists are talking about when they refer to the speed of light is the speed of light in a vacuum, such as in outer space. This speed, referred to as c, is 983,571,057 feet per second.

Why is it impossible to travel faster than the speed of light in a vacuum? The answer is Einstein's famous equation $E=mc^2$ (see page 124). This equation shows how mass (m) and energy (E) are equivalent. It means that the bigger something is, the more energy is locked up inside it.

Crucially, it also means that the more energy something has, the heavier it is. Motion is a type of energy (called kinetic energy), so something that is moving is a tiny bit heavier than something that is at rest. If you throw a baseball at 100 mph, the ball gets 0.000000000002 g heavier.

This is a tiny amount, but as your speed gets closer to the speed of light, the increase in mass becomes enormous. A spaceship traveling at 90 percent of the speed of light is twice as massive as the same ship at rest. This means the engines have to work twice as hard to make it go faster. But the faster it goes, the more energy it has and the more massive it becomes, and so the more energy you have to put in to speed it up. Meanwhile, everything inside the ship is also getting heavier; the watch on your wrist, which used to weigh about 0.49 oz, would now weigh about 36 tons.

A spaceship reaching the speed of light would become infinitely heavy and would need an infinite amount of energy to move. Obviously, this is impossible. This is why nothing can go as fast as—let alone faster than—the speed of light.

The top speed attained by human technology was over 150,000 mph, by the spacecraft Helios 2.

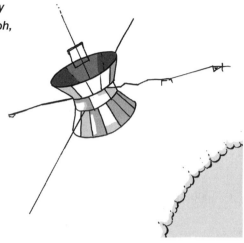

There are some ways around this problem. Some scientists think that particles with no mass such as tachyons could travel faster than light. The speed of light is their slowest possible speed. However, these are purely hypothetical particles and may not exist at all.

It might be possible to get to a distant star faster than a ray of light if you had some way of skipping the space in between. If you could fold or warp space, you could jump from one place to another without crossing the intervening distance. Perhaps it might be possible to go through a wormhole in the fabric of space-time.

Why is there no life on Mars?

There is no life on Mars because it is too cold and dry, as it has almost no plate tectonics and thus does not benefit from the greenhouse effect.

There may have been life on Mars in the past, when it was warmer and wetter, and there may still be life in Mars, below the surface. But there is almost certainly no life on the surface of the Red Planet.

The immediate reason for this is that it is too cold and dry. The temperature at the surface ranges from about -207°F to about 98°F, but even when it is above 32°F, water cannot exist as a liquid because the pressure is so low. The Martian atmosphere is 100 times thinner than Earth's, so any liquid water would instantly boil away into gas.

The distance of Mars from the sun is similar to that of Earth; if it had a thicker atmosphere, like ours, the greenhouse effect might keep it warm enough for liquid water and sustainable life.

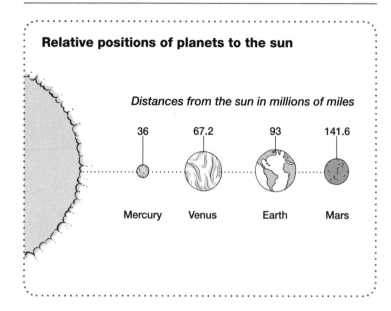

Relative positions of planets to the sun

Distances from the sun in millions of miles

36	67.2	93	141.6
Mercury	Venus	Earth	Mars

A few billion years ago, Mars probably had a thicker atmosphere. The thing is, Mars is much smaller than Earth and has weaker gravity, meaning that its atmosphere probably leaked into space.

The lack of life on the planet could also point to the minimal amount of plate tectonics on Mars. On Earth, plate tectonics help maintain a constant level of carbon dioxide, the most important greenhouse gas, in the atmosphere. When water is around, falling as rain or splashing around in the oceans, carbon dioxide dissolves into the water and chemically reacts with rocks. This reaction forms rocks such as chalk and limestone, and the carbon is locked away. Plate tectonics suck these rocks down into the planet's hot interior, melt them, and then blast the carbon back out into the atmosphere through volcanoes. Thanks to plate tectonics, there is a carbon cycle.

On Mars, there are almost no plate tectonics, and thus, a minimal carbon cycle. When it was warmer and wetter, carbon dioxide in the Martian atmosphere was locked away in rocks through similar processes to those found on Earth, but then it was locked away forever. The more carbon dioxide that was removed, the less of a greenhouse effect there was and the colder it got. The colder it got, the more water condensed out of the atmosphere as rain, and the more carbon dioxide was removed. It was a runaway reverse greenhouse effect, and the result was a cold, dry, barren planet.

Hot and heavy

Almost exactly the opposite happened on Venus. Venus is almost the same size as Earth, and billions of years ago, it too may have had a gentler, wetter climate. But Venus is just a little bit closer to the sun than Earth, and instead of water falling as rain, it stayed in the atmosphere as steam and triggered a mammoth greenhouse effect. The heat released masses of carbon dioxide from the rocks, and now Venus has a crushingly thick, unbearably hot atmosphere. The surface air pressure is 92 times higher than on Earth, so walking on the surface of Venus would be like walking on Earth's ocean bottom 1,000 yards down, except that the temperature is nearly 900°F, hot enough to melt lead!

Another reason tectonic activity is important to life on Earth is that life may well have started around a hydrothermal vent, a sort of water volcano on the bottom of the ocean. The best place to look for life elsewhere in the universe may be around similar vents; for instance, there might be some on Europa, the sixth moon of Jupiter.

Why is the moon the same apparent size as the sun?

The moon is the same apparent size as the sun because even though the sun is 400 times wider than the moon, it is also 400 times farther away.

Why is there such a remarkable similarity between the size and distance of the moon and the sun? It's simply a coincidence.

This incredible coincidence is unique among all the planets in the solar system and all 166 of their (known) moons. So far, it is unique even among all the other planets discovered in the galaxy.

Thanks to this coincidence, the earth witnesses a total eclipse when the moon passes directly in front of the sun, blacking out its disc and leaving only the corona (the extended outer atmosphere of the sun) visible.

Total eclipses are rare because the moon is not always the same apparent size as the sun. Both the moon and the earth have elliptical orbits (i.e., not perfectly circular), so the moon usually looks a bit smaller than the sun, leading to what is called an annular eclipse.

Ever since it formed, the moon has been moving farther away from the earth. Today it is moving about 1.5 inches farther away every year, so if you are 50 years old, the moon is more than 6 feet farther away from the planet than when you were born.

As the moon moves away, it gets smaller in the sky, which means that the moon and sun did not match up perfectly in the past and will stop matching up at some point in the future. The type of total eclipse we witness today, with its spectacular and awe-inspiring corona, could not be seen in the past, and will no longer be possible around 1.5 billion years in the future.

It seems that humans are incredibly lucky to be around at exactly the right time to see total eclipses of the sun. But is it just a coincidence? One possibility put forward is that total eclipses are involved in human evolution; in this case, it would not be a coincidence at all.

Why does my cell phone lose its signal?

Your cell phone loses its signal for a variety of reasons: Because you move away from the cell tower, buildings and hills get in the way, other people steal your signal, and signals can interfere with one another.

A cell phone is basically a walkie-talkie, except that it doesn't talk directly with other phones; it has to go through a cell tower in order to communicate. Each tower broadcasts radio signals over relatively small cells, or areas. The strength of your signal, and whether you lose that signal altogether, depends on how well your phone can swap radio signals with a tower.

There are many different factors involved in deciding how well your phone and the tower can swap signals: distance, number of people in the area trying to make calls, your network, your phone, the geography of your surroundings, and luck.

Each tower has limited power, so it can only cover a limited range. It also has a limited number of slots available for use, so if all the slots are taken up, your phone will try to connect with a tower that is farther away.

This will make a serious dent in your signal strength, because the power at which radio waves are transmitted by a tower drops off as the inverse square of distance. This means that if you have to connect with a tower twice as far away, its signal strength will be four times weaker.

When a signal leaves the tower, it has around 20 watts of power, but by the time it reaches your phone, it usually has just a millionth or a billionth of a watt of power. In other words, getting bumped out to a more distant tower is bad news.

The weakness of the signal from the tower is also a serious problem if you are inside a building, behind a tree, or under water. Weak signals are easily blocked by brick, concrete, glass, rock, and water.

With signals bouncing all over the place and reflecting off various objects, especially in the city, you could have signals arriving at your phone from all directions at once. These signals are radio waves, and waves can interfere with each other. The trough of one wave can cancel out the peak of another, weakening your signal even more.

Weather can also affect your signal strength. Rain and storms weaken the signals and interfere with your phone's reception. Even the way you hold your phone might affect its efficiency, as iPhone users found to their cost during the "death grip" furor that greeted the launch of the iPhone 4.

APPENDIX

Selected References

AeroSpaceGuide: aerospaceguide.net

Ask a Scientist: askascientist.com

Astronomy magazine: astronomy.com

Astronomy Notes: astronomynotes.com

Environmental Protection Agency: epa.gov

Eric Weisstein's World of Science: scienceworld.wolfram.com

Eureka! The National Children's Museum: eureka.org.uk

Extreme Science: extremescience.com

The Human Touch of Chemistry: humantouchofchemistry.com

Hypertextbook: hypertextbook.com

Mad Sci Network: madsci.org

Matter: matter.org.uk

Met Office: metoffice.gov.uk

NASA: science.nasa.gov

National Center for Biotechnology Information: ncbi.nlm.nih.gov

National Geographic: nationalgeographic.com

National Institutes of Health, Office of Science Education:
    science.education.nih.gov

National Oceanography Centre: www.pol.ac.uk

National Sleep Research Project:
    www.abc.net.au/science/sleep/facts.htm

Nature: nature.com

NewScientist magazine: newscientist.com

Newton, Ask a Scientist, DOE Office of Science:
newton.dep.anl.gov

Nine Planets: nineplanets.org

NOAA: www.noaa.gov

Nuclear Energy Institute: www.nei.org

Office of Scientific & Technical Information: osti.gov

OUP blog: blog.oup.com

The Particle Adventure: particleadventure.org

PBS NOVA: pbs.org/wgbh/nova

Plus magazine: plus.maths.org

Programmed Aging Theory Info: programmed-aging.org

Psychology Today magazine: psychologytoday.com

ScienceDaily: sciencedaily.com

Science magazine of the American Association for the
Advancement of Science: sciencemag.org

Scientific American magazine: sciam.com

Scripps Institution of Oceanography, Explorations Now:
explorations.ucsd.edu

Society for Popular Astronomy: popastro.com

Stanford Encyclopedia of Philosophy: plato.stanford.edu

The Straight Dope: straightdope.com

The Tech Museum: thetech.org

Universe Today: universetoday.com

University of Illinois Physics Van: van.physics.illinois.edu

U.S. Geological Survey: usgs.gov

Wired Science: wired.com/wiredscience

Bibliography

American Heritage Science Dictionary, The (Houghton Mifflin Harcourt, 2005)

Banks, William P. (ed.), *Encyclopedia of Consciousness* (Elsevier, 2009)

Chown, Marcus, *Quantum Theory Cannot Hurt You: A Guide to the Universe* (Faber and Faber, 2007)

Comins, Neil, *What If the Earth Had Two Moons?: And Nine Other Thought-Provoking Speculations on the Solar System* (St. Martins Press, 2010)

Cullerne, John (ed.), *Penguin Dictionary of Physics*, Fourth Edition (Penguin, 2009)

Davey, Graham, *Encyclopaedic Dictionary of Psychology* (Hodder Education, 2006)

Diamond, Jared, *Guns, Germs, and Steel: A Short History of Everybody for the Last 13,000 Years* (Vintage, 2005)

Hartson, William, *The Things That Nobody Knows: 501 Mysteries of Life, the Universe, and Everything* (Atlantic Books, 2011)

McFadden, Lucy-Ann, Weissman, Paul R. & Johnson, Torrence V. (eds), *Encyclopedia of the Solar System* (Elsevier, 2007)

Levy, Joel, *Scientific Feuds: From Galileo to the Human Genome* (New Holland Publishers, 2010)

Levy, Joel, *The Doomsday Book: Scenarios for the End of the World* (Vision Paperbacks, 2005)

Matthews, Robert, *Why Don't Spiders Stick to Their Webs?: And Other Everyday Mysteries of Science* (Oneworld Publications, 2007)

McGraw-Hill Concise Encyclopedia of Science and Technology, Sixth Edition (McGraw-Hill Professional, 2009)

Moore, Patrick (ed.), *Philip's Astronomy Encyclopedia* (BCA, 2002)

Pernetta, John, *Philip's Guide to the Oceans* (Philips, 2004)

Pinet, Paul R., *Invitation to Oceanography* (Jones and Bartlett, 2009)

Roeckelein, J. (ed.), *Dictionary of Psychological Theories* (Elsevier, 2006)

Index

INDEX

V

veins 71
color of 72
Venus 161
volcanic eruptions 38, 40–1, 56–8, 174

W

Waialeale 65
water
 breathing under 87–9
 and cell phone reception 180
 comparison of with electricity 154
 composition of 27
 conversion with carbon dioxide into sugar 15
 cycle 65
 density of 125, 128–30
 freezing of 22–3
 and ice's buoyancy 7, 8, 163–16
 lack of in liquid form on Mars 173
 molecules of 22–3
 apparent movement of during tides 24
 oxygen in 23, 27, 87–9

percentage of Earth covered by 142
 role of in carbon cycle 174–5
 role in plant reproduction 35
 role in photosynthesis 32, 111
 role in rusting 30
 as rain 63–5
 on Venus 175
 see also sea
weather
 hurricanes 39, 145
 rain 63–5
 tornadoes 145
 wind 143–5, 144
 see also temperature
weight
 and buoyancy 128–30
 of water 128–30
wind 143–5, 144
 highest recorded speed of 145
 see also air; hurricanes; tornadoes

Y

year
duration of 19–21
on other planets 19